RAYMOND KRMASCHEK III
PATHWAYS
TO SPIRITUALITY

WE ARE ALL ONE

PATHWAYS TO SPIRITUALITY
WE ARE ALL ONE

iUniverse books may be ordered through booksellers or by contacting:

iUniverse
1663 Liberty Drive
Bloomington, IN 47403
www.iuniverse.com
1-800-Authors (1-800-288-4677)

ISBN: 978-1-5320-3640-8 (sc)
ISBN: 978-1-5320-3641-5 (e)

Library of Congress Control Number: 2017917742

Print information available on the last page.

iUniverse rev. date: 11/10/2017

Foreword

Welcome to pathways to spiritualism … a guide for the beginner and an aid for those already moving along their Path … I'm sure you already took a look at the book and said, this makes no sence to me … well that would have to do on how you use it … most spiritual books will somewhere in it tell you what to do or how to act and what to believe … .this would be like Sunday school in a church … would it not???my book will nowhere tell you any of those things … you see …, I believe as many others that all answers either lie within you or at your fingertips from the Higher Power … and you probably use different names for the same thing … .no my friends, this book will make you open your minds and use them to find your own answers and if just starting, your own path or journey ….

Everyone has their own journey in life and paths may cross where we learn more information, but still it's your own personal journey …

so your still wondering how this book can help you … well for yrs now I have been accumulating questions and my comments, in order for people to read and come up with answers of their own to create their path or help on theirs … you see no one can TELL you how to have a path or journey, even though all those books you paid for say they can … and, everytime you read a question you will have to think of answers(((sounds like work,,,well it is,,,for your mind)))) and as you do your mind will expand more and you will see a way you would like to proceed with your journey or path … I will even guarantee that before you can finish this book, you will have went back and maybe even changed your previous answers … .now the questions and comments are written in such a way because they were posed to thousands over many yrs..But you will get them very quickly … check some out … And great luck on finding or enhancing your Path and Journey..

Ray.

Question:::::to be a soul, or not to be, that is the question … not really just wanted to get your attention for this multi question … .a little humor here … lol … now I believe a soul is inserted into a being upon conception..and I also believe all souls are pure at first … SOME, people say murderers and rapists and child molesters and etc., all have no soul..I say every living being has a soul..those types of people have a dark soul … I don't believe we choose our life before … we come back..we have choices and free will … if you believe that you have already chosen your future then you need no free will and can do anything you want, good or evil, with no consequences … .or you might as well just end your life if you have no choice on how to live it … then again, maybe that's the reason you came back..to commit suicide or kill people, or rape them … you see, I don't believe any of that … so, my question is:::::::do you believe a soul comes to you pure, and if so what things can change it to darkness??????

Comment::::now that I have put out there the possibility to change vibration and see things not meant for the normal sences ... I will say by a close relationship with your Higher Power, you can see whatever you want without changing anything ... .just my belief

Question:::::a lot of people say they get their guidance and answers in many ways … angels, spirits, etc … now I don't doubt that at all … but my simple question is why not just talk to the Higher Power and eliminate the middle men???????

_____
_____
_____
_____
_____
_____
_____
_____
_____
_____
_____
_____
_____
_____
_____
_____
_____
_____
_____
_____
_____
_____
_____
_____
_____
_____
_____
_____
_____
_____

Question:::::now there has been a fellow on some of my groups who has said some interesting things about the killing of livestock and trees and the such … .at one point he said if a butcher kills for food it is not against the Karma … this got me thinking, smell the smoke.lolol … this should also be of interest to those who say they are vegetarians … now these are only my beliefs, and am looking forward to yours, after the question … I do believe that ALL living things have a s … oul..but on the other hand we do also and have to eat to survive … we are not termites who live on dead wood after all … we need meat and vegetables … and we kill them to eat and survive … now we must look at this in a spiritual perspective … we are also animals … since the beginning of man we lived off the land eating anything we could to survive, and still do … my question is:::::do we have to worry about Karma and its consequences by doing this, or is it an exeption to the rule of killing????????

_____

_____

_____

_____

_____

_____

_____

_____

_____

_____

_____

_____

_____

_____

_____

_____

_____

_____

_____

_____

_____

_____

question::::::::since according to one of my recent questions, most believe there can be no mortal Master of spirituality on this earth ..and I hope we all spiritual people strive to have understanding and knowledge while were here. my question is:::::will there come a time before you pass on that you can say your truly happy with your knowledge and ability to help others, or will you go out with something inside you empty?????????

_____
_____
_____
_____
_____
_____
_____
_____
_____
_____
_____
_____
_____
_____
_____
_____
_____
_____
_____
_____
_____
_____
_____
_____
_____
_____
_____
_____
_____
_____
_____
_____

Question::::now we all have our own idea of what the Higher Power is … .but here's a scenario to get you thinking … .If all at once huge spaceships, appeared out of no where above all the capitals of the world and wanted to speak to our leaders … and there message was … we have come back. We were the ones who seeded you humans on this planet along with everything else … this is only our corporial showing of us … we are actually beings that are made of light … we have b … een listening to all of you and your wants and needs and have taken action for what's best for you … we see how you have lived your lives and it seems to be directed in the way of self destruction … .we don't want to take any action against any of you because we believe you all have the ability to correct things … you all know what is needed … we will be leaving soon and let you go on your paths and hope you can all live together … this is the reason for our return and message … .we will be back in the future so spread the word to your children and their children … now my question is::::::would you consider them to be the Higher Power, or believe their is one Higher then them who really is in control?????

_____
_____
_____
_____
_____
_____
_____
_____
_____
_____
_____
_____
_____
_____
_____
_____
_____
_____
_____
_____
_____
_____

Questions::::yes plural..I am going to try something a little different today with this post ... usually, I blab a lot and then get to the question..and I am very happy with the feedback comments on my groups..but today I will be blabbing.lol and have more then one question within this post ... I am trying to get more people responding to my posts by doing this with more then one question ... so let's see what happens ... vibrations ... .everyone and everything has a different one, but ..., some are so close together that we can see and hear the other things that are close to our vibration ... take the earth for example ... it has a vibration soooo close to all living things on it we can see them ... question:::::;do you believe this last statement or do you have a different opinion?????now again, our vibration is such that there are certain things we can't see or hear ... for instance, demons and angels ... if we could change our vibration to theirs or theirs to ours would we be able to see them and them us and communicate?????and then again can being in a certain state of vibration protect us from the darkness and let in the light???????

Question:::::now my dream has been always to live in a community of spiritual people … living independently from the world around us … that's not to say we could not be friends with people nearby and maybe even trade with them … like some of the movies, but without the mistakes they made..lol … we might be even called a commune, but we would never show ourselves to be any cult in any way … the Mormons do it!!!!well I don't think I'll live to see it, but maybe it will happen someday and grow to be something great … my question is::::how many out there would be willing to give up everything they have to be a part of it???????

question::::you all can believe what you want to and live in your personal worlds until you pass on … .doesn't really matter … you may change one or two little things while here … but you will never be a part of the BIG change until you all unite under a common cause … my question is ::::will you take that step to do it??????

Question:::::now it is my personal opinion that those who claim to be witches, have a long line of heritage that dates back centuries as do the other spiritual peoples as the pagans and gnostics and the druids and more … for the most part they are spiritual and good. But because of things that happened in times ago they have been given a bad name … .but most of you are afraid still to see their light and so you make them hide. When they can be of great strength in communion with the spiritual of today … my wife was one who ran her own covent at one time until she decided to become a solitary … I still keep up her alter … my question is :::::why do you spiritual always say you don't judge but do it every day to people like them???????

_____
_____
_____
_____
_____
_____
_____
_____
_____
_____
_____
_____
_____
_____
_____
_____
_____
_____
_____
_____
_____
_____
_____
_____
_____
_____

Question:::::well, there is a saying that goes something like this (give a man a fish and he will eat for a day, teach a man to fish and he can eat forever) … .now I have a parable..there was a village that was near a fresh water lake and were hunters,,,but didn't know anything about fishing … one day a man was walking down the beach with 2 big baskets full of fish..there were about 6 men sitting on the beach..one asked, what was in the baskets and the man replied, I have brought … for you some fish for your people to eat tonight … they took the baskets and went back to their village … the next day the man was sitting on the beach and another from the village approached..he asked how the man had so many fish and where did they come from..the first said I caught them. It is called fishing … well the first asked if he would teach him to fish … the man asked why and he said so that he could teach his village and they would all be able to eat all the time … so the man taught him and he went on his way … several months later he returned to the village and found that the man had taught no one to fish but instead caught all the fish himself and traded for them until he was the richest of the village … so thinking about this story my question is:::::how do you really know who you should help or teach that will use the knowledge you give them for the betterment of all??????

_____
_____
_____
_____
_____
_____
_____
_____
_____
_____
_____
_____
_____
_____
_____
_____
_____
_____
_____
_____

now many people have many different gifts … some more then one … and some none at all … some are learning them and some are afraid of them..my question to you is:::::what do you believe to be the most powerful gift one can have???????

_____
_____
_____
_____
_____
_____
_____
_____
_____
_____
_____
_____
_____
_____
_____
_____
_____
_____
_____
_____
_____
_____
_____
_____
_____
_____
_____
_____
_____
_____

Question:::::and this is not in any way starting a fight ..I truly would like to hear an answer ... for the religious on the groups, and there are many, but don't ramble on about it ... this question has bothered me for yrs ... no book or priest or reverend has ever been able to answer it ... now there are different types of dark or evil people on this earth..some way nastier then others ... from a simple thief to a mass murderer ... My question is::::when they die and go to hell, how long do they have to be punished depending on their crimes??????you know I don't believe in heaven or hell but am still curious what you think in your beliefs

_____
_____
_____
_____
_____
_____
_____
_____
_____
_____
_____
_____
_____
_____
_____
_____
_____
_____
_____
_____
_____
_____
_____
_____
_____

Question:::::Now I believe that ALL living things have a soul, or spirit, or life force … whatever you want to call it … but I also believe that All living things were born spiritual with the connection to the Higher Power … we see this in animals all the time..they only do what is necessary to survive … they don't kill for sport and even nurture other types of animals occasionally … beside their own … in the ecosystem of the ocean we see all the time how species coexist need … ing each other to survive … don't ask me why humans fell off that path, and turned to violence for no reason and abuse and taking advantage of each other … but, we are trying to change that back now..and as you know it's no easy task … but my question is:::::do you think the size of a species, as a plant or animal has a different type of soul or spirit or life force then we do, or less or more, or are all our souls equal??????

Question::::now I don't know about the rest of you but being spiritual is as easy as having a cup of coffee in the morning … if you do, you get it though … .EASY … like the song..Easy like Sunday morning … maybe to a lot of you it isn't so easy … I get messages and e-mails all the time asking why they don't get anything for them and claim to be spiritual … well just being spiritual as you think is not the answer … over coffee I will have a chat with my Higher Power … neve … r ask for anything for myself … maybe for others … and you know the very simple secret to having a happy spiritual life is … Belief, TRUE BELIEF … none of this complicated crap trying to figure out what it is..Belief … that's ALL it asks … and the people who message me and e-mail me just don't get it ..they all want something first so that they can believe … ain't gonna happen folks … you gotta give to get, simple … now this is only my system and it works for me … so don't start saying that I think I know it all because I don't really know shit..and if the Higher Power wants me to know it tells me … so my question to you is:::::what aspect of being spiritual works for you???????

_____
_____
_____
_____
_____
_____
_____
_____
_____
_____
_____
_____
_____
_____
_____
_____
_____
_____
_____
_____
_____
_____
_____
_____

Question:::::when I ask a question and someone says a comment to contradict me, if you read closely you will find they end up contradicting themselves ... it's not important unless they see that contradiction ... my questions are only to have people open their minds and comment what they think about the answers ... and you people are doing great because even myself learns as we go along in conversation ... .but remember, being spiritual is also being simple ... at least that's what ... I believe ... we don't need physicists answering the questions with their scientific knowledge and clouding the pathways. And we especially don't need answers that just pose more questions ... one step at a time ... if you believe you have to do that then pose a post with the question ... don't forget peeps, WE are all ONE here and we at Individuals also so the answers won't always agree ... my question is :::::name me one common goal in being spiritual??????

_____
_____
_____
_____
_____
_____
_____
_____
_____
_____
_____
_____
_____
_____
_____
_____
_____
_____
_____
_____
_____

Comment::::now that I have put out there the possibility to change vibration and see things not meant for the normal sences … I will say by a close relationship with your Higher Power, you can see whatever you want without changing anything … .just my belief

Question:::::now my dream has been always to live in a community of spiritual people ... living independently from the world around us ... that's not to say we could not be friends with people nearby and maybe even trade with them ... like some of the movies, but without the mistakes they made..lol ... we might be even called a commune, but we would never show ourselves to be any cult in any way ... the Mormons do it!!!!well I don't think I'll live to see it, but maybe it will happen someday and grow to be something great ... my question is::::how many out there would be willing to give up everything they have to be a part of it???????

Questions::::yes plural..I am going to try something a little different today with this post … usually, I blab a lot and then get to the question..and I am very happy with the feedback comments on my groups..but today I will be blabbing.lol and have more then one question within this post … I am trying to get more people responding to my posts by doing this with more then one question … so let's see what happens … vibrations … .everyone and everything has a different one, but …, some are so close together that we can see and hear the other things that are close to our vibration … take the earth for example … it has a vibration soooo close to all living things on it we can see them … question:::::;do you believe this last statement or do you have a different opinion?????now again, our vibration is such that there are certain things we can't see or hear … for instance, demons and angels … if we could change our vibration to theirs or theirs to ours would we be able to see them and them us and communicate?????and then again can being in a certain state of vibration protect us from the darkness and let in the light???????

_____
_____
_____
_____
_____
_____
_____
_____
_____
_____
_____
_____
_____
_____
_____
_____
_____
_____
_____
_____
_____
_____

Question:::::question and comments … sometimes I post comments ..but if you notice I never say anything like this is the TRUTH … .that's because everyone has their own truth until they meet someone with a similar truth … I always say, this is what I believe … .but for my questions, one of the reasons I post them is to see other spiritual answers so I can grow my personal knowledge and expand and strengthen my path with your answers that are not mine … I always have a personal answer to my questions … remember I said one of my reasons???my question is what do you think the main reason I have for posting my questions????????

_____

_____

_____

_____

_____

_____

_____

_____

_____

_____

_____

_____

_____

_____

_____

_____

_____

_____

_____

_____

_____

_____

_____

_____

_____

Question:::::now I posed a question on here a little while ago ..it was … name me one common goal in being spiritual?????? well I had one member not really answer the question directly, but said something about science and spirituality being connected … .so my question to you now is::::::as much as we know now about science and spirituality,,do you think they are connected at this time as far as we know??????

Question::::::well it appears that many of you believe in science will give you the answers to being spiritual or visa versa … .well my simple question to you is:::::::::do you go with both or choose one at time??????

Show more reactions

_____

_____

_____

_____

_____

_____

_____

_____

_____

_____

_____

_____

_____

_____

_____

_____

_____

_____

_____

_____

_____

_____

_____

_____

_____

_____

_____

_____

Question:::::now one of our members on one of our groups said I should talk about the devil and shake things up … well I will but not the way he thinks … first of, I don't believe in a devil … especially the one from religious books of all religions … but, I will say this … if we are to talk about him, let's use his Angelic name … Lucifer, Morningstar..which means the bringer of light … doesn't sound too spooky does it … one who would bring light to humanity could certainly … not be a being who would make souls suffer … it's a contradiction in itself … .now IF, IF, IF I did believe in a hell, I would think it a place where we would actually be taught the error of our ways and not be tortured … we would be taught how to be more loving and caring and more spiritual as a whole … .this is how I would look at it … my question to you is::::::what would be your Idea of a Hell????????

_____
_____
_____
_____
_____
_____
_____
_____
_____
_____
_____
_____
_____
_____
_____
_____
_____
_____
_____
_____
_____
_____
_____

Question:::::::well it appears that many of you believe in science will give you the answers to being spiritual or visa versa … .well my simple question to you is:::::::::do you go with both or choose one at time??????

Show more reactions

_____
_____
_____
_____
_____
_____
_____
_____
_____
_____
_____
_____
_____
_____
_____
_____
_____
_____
_____
_____
_____
_____
_____
_____
_____
_____
_____
_____

Question::::::well if you follow the teachings of Budda, then you have to accept it in it's entirety. Or if you follow the Dami Lama the same thing goes..or religion also … it's all or nothing … you can't call yourself religious, but pick and choose what you want to take and believe in..you are a catholic you must take the whole shebang, bible and all and believe in it otherwise your not a catholic … now the same goes for being spiritual … it's all or nothing … you can't be following spiritual practices and religion at the same time … so my question to you is:::::being spiritual is there something about it you don't agree with and why??????

_____
_____
_____
_____
_____
_____
_____
_____
_____
_____
_____
_____
_____
_____
_____
_____
_____
_____
_____
_____
_____
_____
_____
_____

question::::now some of you spiritual people out there believe in alternate dimentions or universes … and, that movement through these dimentions or realities, happens every day … for instance, have you ever woken up and very soon noticed something different..and, I mean physicaly..maybe something out of order that is different then before you went to sleep … and maybe just a feeling that things are different then normal … .something telling you that something has changed … well my question is::::could it be you have changed places with your alternate self while you slept??????

_____

_____

_____

_____

_____

_____

_____

_____

_____

_____

_____

_____

_____

_____

_____

_____

_____

_____

_____

_____

_____

_____

_____

_____

_____

_____

_____

_____

_____

_____

Question::::now all spiritual people do not think 100% alike ... yes we have our core values ..and these are surely what makes us one ... now some of us believe in reincarnation ... and some do not ... some believe we go back to our Higher Power, and some believe we never go there but somewhere else to make our next move ... well I believe when we leave this body, we do go back to our Higher Power and then make decisions on what we want to do ... .I personally don't want to come back, unless it's absolutely necessary ... my question is what do you think happens to your Life Force or soul or spirit when you no longer inhabit your Human form????????

_____
_____
_____
_____
_____
_____
_____
_____
_____
_____
_____
_____
_____
_____
_____
_____
_____
_____
_____
_____
_____
_____
_____

Question::::now all spiritual people do not think 100% alike … yes we have our core values ..and these are surely what makes us one … now some of us believe in reincarnation … and some do not … some believe we go back to our Higher Power, and some believe we never go there but somewhere else to make our next move … well I believe when we leave this body, we do go back to our Higher Power and then make decisions on what we want to do … .I personally don't want to come back, unless it's absolutely necessary … my question is what do you think happens to your Life Force or soul or spirit when you no longer inhabit your Human form????????

Question:::::now all spiritual people do not think 100% alike … yes we have our core values ..and these are surely what makes us one … now some of us believe in reincarnation … and some do not … some believe we go back to our Higher Power, and some believe we never go there but somewhere else to make our next move … well I believe when we leave this body, we do go back to our Higher Power and then make decisions on what we want to do … .I personally don't want to come back, unless it's absolutely necessary … my question is what do you think happens to your Life Force or soul or spirit when you no longer inhabit your Human form????????

_____
_____
_____
_____
_____
_____
_____
_____
_____
_____
_____
_____
_____
_____
_____
_____
_____
_____
_____
_____
_____
_____
_____
_____
_____

Question:::::soo many kinds for soo many reasons … can't even begin to name them..but today I'm more interested in self punishment … people beat them selves up all the time for all kinds of reasons … I didn't do that right. He or she doesn't love me anymore … and on and on and on … .why do we continue to hurt and abuse, and punish ourselves because of someone elses thinking … I thought we were spiritual and on OWN path. Not someone elses … .well for many, I guess not … .we weren't put here to punish ourselves for anything … if mistakes are made then we learn, that's all and don't do it again … so my question to you is::::what do you punish yourself for?????

Question::::If there were a satan..as the bible calls him as Lucifer Morningstar, otherwise know as the bringer of light … he has been helping mankind since adam and eve … per the bible, god created them and put them in the garden of eden and told them they could do as they please,,except,, don't eat from the tree of knowledge … then we have satan appear and talk eve into eating an apple and having adam eat also … BOOM, they can see they are naked, and now aquire knowledge … … .but god in his HOLY forgiveness, banishes them from the garden and it's all down hill from there … what did the Archangel do but bring light to the first children of god … not a bad thing I would say … even in the bible satans name is rarely mentioned … now being spiritual I have no need of any devil..but the religious need it to keep them in line like what happened to adam and eve … disobey me and their will be consequences … lolol … .my question is :::if we are spiritual, and disobey the spiritual ways,,, what happens to us??????

_____
_____
_____
_____
_____
_____
_____
_____
_____
_____
_____
_____
_____
_____
_____
_____
_____
_____
_____
_____
_____
_____

Question:::::well, there is a saying that goes something like this (give a man a fish and he will eat for a day, teach a man to fish and he can eat forever) … .now I have a parable..there was a village that was near a fresh water lake and were hunters,,, but didn't know anything about fishing … one day a man was walking down the beach with 2 big baskets full of fish..there were about 6 men sitting on the beach..one asked, what was in the baskets and the man replied, I have brough … t for you some fish for your people to eat tonight … they took the baskets and went back to their village … the next day the man was sitting on the beach and another from the village approached..he asked how the man had so many fish and where did they come from..the first said I caught them. It is called fishing … well the first asked if he would teach him to fish … the man asked why and he said so that he could teach his village and they would all be able to eat all the time … so the man taught him and he went on his way … several months later he returned to the village and found that the man had taught no one to fish but instead caught all the fish himself and traded for them until he was the richest of the village … so thinking about this story my question is:::::how do you really know who you should help or teach that will use the knowledge you give them for the betterment of all??????

Question::::people .people .people … when will you let go of your own fears of your own beliefs … being so distant from reality that you are nothing more then a sheeple to your own beliefs … don't you want to live your own life as you wish and have your children do the same … someone older and wiser then me once told me,,,,when you do something that you never did before and your scared to do it … after you have done it and found that is was not anywhere as bad as you thought it would be … did that not give you a sense of control over your own destiny to a certain extent … and a feeling so awesome you would do it again in a second … my question is::::are you willing to leave your beliefs and the fear that comes with today???????

Question:::::now all belief systems have rules..these are layed down and followed for a reason ... to ensure unity and make sure nothing bad is being done ... some even have books that lay out these rules and what is needed to be a part of that group ... but what I see on my groups is a non-cohesive bunch of people who all have their own individual spirituality ... this is fine as long as we follow simple rules..like never harm another and always have love and compassion for others, and so on and on ... but, we must start to act in unity for the future of spirituality ... my question is:::do we have to go as far as having some sort of book to both teach us and set down guidelines for being spiritual?????just a question folks, don't bite my head off. I believe we don't need one ...

question::::now some of you spiritual people out there believe in alternate dimentions or universes … and, that movement through these dimentions or realities, happens every day … for instance,,have you ever woken up and very soon noticed something different..and, I mean physicaly..maybe something out of order that is different then before you went to sleep … and maybe just a feeling that things are different then normal … .something telling you that something has changed … well my question is::::could it be you have changed places with your alternate self while you slept??????

Well a word of truth … I have been following for some years now the numbers of people in different belief systems … you can go and check out my fact easily if you choose to … in the world of faith and belief systems in the last 10 yrs. The catholic and Christian religions have been declining at a amazing rate … for every new believer((((and there usually young children)))10 more leave the faith … churches are closing at an alarming rate … not enough people to sustain the chu … rches as needed … .and of those 10 about half are becoming spiritual and the rest are on the fence searching for something new … … .but the spiritual numbers are growing at an amazing rate … no one seems to want to leave?????, even the evangelical, like the jehovah witnesses are disappearing … most of you on my groups are spiritual,,,but there are handful of religious (((and I don't understand why there even here))) that say they are spiritual and religious at the same time … that's a no-no.lolol … you can't play both sides of the fence … hedging your bets..why don't you just make up your minds and choose?????anyway I just thought I would throw that out there for all of you to think about …

life is simple like being spiritual if you want it to be … .you can waste all your time contemplating the questions for the answers … but ultimately the answers lye right at your front door … just open your heart and mind and soul …

question:::::now I know that some of you out there reading this question are religious and some of you believe you can be both religious and spiritual … not a big thing … when I was much younger I was a religious person … then for reasons that no longer are important I lost my faith … for a time I had nothing … no religion, no spiritualism … and I did some awfull things in my life..then one day I seen the light of being spiritual … and as I progressed I found out about Karma … … now I knew it wasn't any good to ask my old god or my newer Higher Power for forgiveness … I realized I had to deal with Karma to make things right … it took many years of being righteous to make things right and believe me it was no picnic … it was like a living hell to make things right … but I had no other choice if I was to continue on a spiritual path.and now when I pose questions here I have to think of all the answers that are possible before I post, and I also from you learn different ones also … so my question is … how do you save your own soul??????

_____
_____
_____
_____
_____
_____
_____
_____
_____
_____
_____
_____
_____
_____
_____
_____
_____
_____
_____
_____
_____
_____

Question::::now religion talks about angels. But in many belief systems they also believe in angels ... in religion they were created by a god of some sort ... question,,, If you believe in angels on the spiritual plane,, what do you think they are and where did they come from?????

_____
_____
_____
_____
_____
_____
_____
_____
_____
_____
_____
_____
_____
_____
_____
_____
_____
_____
_____
_____
_____
_____
_____
_____
_____
_____
_____
_____
_____
_____

Question::::now I believe there are 2 energies that we have..one is the body itself that needs to be filled all the time … consumption of food will give us that … the other is an energy that resides within the shell we call the body but connected to it … this I will call life force, or spirit or soul … now as the other the life force can run down in energy also … for instance,, when used to do a healing it takes some of that energy … my question is :::how do you get new energy and where do you get it???????

_____

_____

_____

_____

_____

_____

_____

_____

_____

_____

_____

_____

_____

_____

_____

_____

_____

_____

_____

_____

_____

_____

_____

_____

_____

_____

question:::I personally believe there is a difference between religion and being spiritual … In religion, you go to a building that looks all pretty and sit and stand and kneel and pray and feed the basket … all while having to follow the way of the book that is the word for you to follow … let's use catholics and Christians for instance … you must follow the word of your bible or else when you die you go to a Hell … or you can repent every time you … go there and be absolved of your previous sins by doing some sort of restitution … maybe some hail Mary's or our father … or a donation to the church … no free will there … on the other hand, being spiritual we have no book to follow … no payment of any kind for committing sins because we just make mistakes and learn and move forward … .we have free will to do as we please as long as it is in love, peace and compassion, amongst other things, all good … my question is do you think you can be religious and spiritual at the same time??????

_____

_____

_____

_____

_____

_____

_____

_____

_____

_____

_____

_____

_____

_____

_____

_____

_____

_____

_____

_____

_____

_____

_____

_____

Question:::we talked here about what it is to be spiritual … .this I would like to propose to you that's a little different..maybe even off the path … grudges,, we maybe all,,, some kind or the other … maybe something from long ago that we still hold in our subconscience … somethin that we never think about anymore … but we never look for them because it's been soooo long ago our mind doesn't remember … but it's still there..my question is … Is forgiveness the answer if we find them or maybe just putting it back away to get rid of it in our mind …???????

Question:::OK I talked a little before about the very old day of the black plaque … .some weren't effected,,,some got sick,,,and some died … it was all because of the genes we had … read about it if you don't believe me … .well I think that this might be coming again … our world is overpopulated according to some … and there are many factions who want to do this now … not about race or origins but just plain old deleting most of the population … .sounds, crazy … but I … feel it's coming … one way or the other ..mankind will create it's own apocalypse … .go ahead and think I'm crazy … enjoy yourself now … but watch the signs and when there ready they will do it … we will destroy ourselves … I know,,, I have seen it,,,and now I no longer,, being spiritual,,, am scared … … laugh at me now but I have never lied to you before … you will feel it coming but it will be too late … but it will not effect the spiritual ones … because we are the ones to be left to have the world to us … and have a new start … you can think me crazy,, but I have never lied to any of you before and not now … It may be beyond some of our time but it will Happen … tell this to your children and teach them to be spiritual … .that is our only hope for our Humanity to continue … .now take time to laugh before the future smacks you in thye head and it's too late … .my question is:::::do you believe me????????

_____
_____
_____
_____
_____
_____
_____
_____
_____
_____
_____
_____
_____
_____
_____
_____
_____
_____
_____

comment::::we talk a lot about being spiritual on the groups here … everyone has there own idea of what it is to be spiritual … well, I believe we ALL have something in common as spiritual people … let me tell you what it is to be spiritual from my point of view … I am spiritual because I have a total overwhelming love for ALL living things on this planet,,and also have the abundant need to share this feeling with all that I can and will accept it … very simple as it should be … no theatrics,,no mind boggling crap,,,just a very simple thing … this I believe is the basic platform from spiritual people have there start … if you don't agree, that's fine … maybe I'm wrong?????

Question::::I know we have talked about Karma before, but I would like to revisit it from a different perspective … we know what Karma does..it punishes the guilty and rewards the good … but,,my question is,,do you think Karma was created by the Higher Power,,or do we create it as we go along in life??????

_____

_____

_____

_____

_____

_____

_____

_____

_____

_____

_____

_____

_____

_____

_____

_____

_____

_____

_____

_____

_____

_____

_____

_____

_____

_____

_____

_____

question::::now first I want to say that you can't be religious and spiritual at the same time … you can't cover your bets..this isn't like gambling … lolol … now I would like to say I believe that the different sects, just mention a few here,, are wiccans, gnostics,,pagans,, druids are a few of what I would consider spiritual people … my question is,,are you one of these groups and would you agree??????

_____
_____
_____
_____
_____
_____
_____
_____
_____
_____
_____
_____
_____
_____
_____
_____
_____
_____
_____
_____
_____
_____
_____
_____
_____
_____
_____
_____
_____

Question:::::spirituality and rocket science ... first of all I would like to tell all those who believe themselves to be spiritual would never want to live in the here and now..I personaly live in the past and the present and the future so I can always move forward ... this is not complicated once you have achieved the understanding of how it's done ... but my real intent with this post is to ask why some people who claim to be spiritual have to try and make the answers we seek ... so complicated ... .for instance,,take us away from this world for a moment,, all mankind and watch and see how spiritual deals with all else that's left ... amazing if you think about it ... there is an order to things,, now put us back into the equation and wham ... we screw it all up ... why, because we are not all spiritual ... we are moving forward but at a slow pace, And I believe the world needs us but not now are they ready ... but why do some people have the need to make, or understand being spiritual as a complicated thing ... I have seen here on my spiritual groups people trying to explain it through geometry, math, religion, and all the other sciences ... Instead of just accepting it for what it is ... my question is,,,do you believe being spiritual should be simple, with simple answers???????

_____

_____

_____

_____

_____

_____

_____

_____

_____

_____

_____

_____

_____

_____

_____

_____

_____

_____

_____

_____

_____

Question:::::::why is it that anyone who does whats called majik, is considered a witch ... and as soon as they are they are considered evil or bad or dark ... .I have been casting spells for many a year and I don't consider myself a witch or bad or evil ... ... I may be called a spell caster..but all my powers I have come from the Higher Power..no one has ever been able to attack me successfully in a spiritual way ... and you also could be like that with the help of the Higher Power ... it's called being spiritual ... but you have to achieve a certain level ... and if you read my post on what it takes to be spiritual, really, down to earth spiritual you would understand ... my question is,,,how many of you out there can say they are ready to truly be spiritual??????and for the rest who say they already are for their own reasons ... good for you

Question::::now it makes sence that you all on this group consider yourselves to be spiritual … .you may post spiritual things, and never say anything about yourself … and that is fine … Also being spiritual to people will always be different … but I believe at the roots core we all believe in something that brings us together … I have my spiritual beliefs, and I will tell you here but not at this time as to not cloud your decisions … my question is:::::what do you think makes you a spiritual person???????what are your beliefs?????if you don't want to put yourself out there on the line I will understand …

_____

_____

_____

_____

_____

_____

_____

_____

_____

_____

_____

_____

_____

_____

_____

_____

_____

_____

_____

_____

_____

_____

_____

_____

_____

Question::::now in this whole world of about 7 billion, we have are rapists, murderers, child molesters and the list goes on and on down the line … we know that all the talking to our Higher power will never solve these things..we still have stupid wars also … and I will be one who says, violence will not solve these problems..violence should only be a last resort in self defence … now I know if you are reading this then you are a spiritual person, and so I ask … … how shall we, the spiritual people, change this world for the better ..and I don't mean one at a time … that would never work, too many people and too long to do it …??????

_____
_____
_____
_____
_____
_____
_____
_____
_____
_____
_____
_____
_____
_____
_____
_____
_____
_____
_____
_____
_____
_____
_____
_____
_____

Question:::::some of you may look at what I'm about to tell you as just crazy … some may not and understand because you have been there … a short while ago I was sitting at my kitchen table..and all of a sudden an evil presence was on the other side attempting to only talk to me … not to attack me in any way … of course I have my protection, but if it's not attacking then it's OK … well it starting reminding me of all the bad things I did in my life and how I was a bad or da … rk person … well I informed it that across time I have made amends for all that I have done and Karmacly speaking I was ahead of the game … … it tried to tell me that once you done something bad that was it … no reprieves … I said it can believe what it wants but I know the truth … IT said I was one of them and there was no escape … well I just chuckled and said … whatever you want to believe you can … I know the truth … after that it disappeared … I loved the experience … I had beaten down the darkness, once again … .as so many times before … my question to you is,,,has anything like this ever happened to you?????????

_____
_____
_____
_____
_____
_____
_____
_____
_____
_____
_____
_____
_____
_____
_____
_____
_____
_____
_____
_____
_____

Question::::now religion talks about angels.but in many belief systems they also believe in angels … in religion they were created by a god of some sort … question,,,If you believe in angels on the spiritual plane,,what do you think they are and where did they come from?????

_____
_____
_____
_____
_____
_____
_____
_____
_____
_____
_____
_____
_____
_____
_____
_____
_____
_____
_____
_____
_____
_____
_____
_____
_____
_____
_____
_____
_____

question:::::now I know that some of you out there reading this question are religious and some of you believe you can be both religious and spiritual ... not a big thing ... when I was much younger I was a religious person ... then for reasons that no longer are important I lost my faith ... for a time I had nothing ... no religion, no spiritualism ... and I did some awfull things in my life..then one day I seen the light of being spiritual ... and as I progressed I found out about Karma ... ... now I knew it wasn't any good to ask my old god or my newer Higher Power for forgiveness ... I realized I had to deal with Karma to make things right ... it took many years of being righteous to make things right and believe me it was no picnic ... it was like a living hell to make things right ... but I had no other choice if I was to continue on a spiritual path.and now when I pose questions here I have to think of all the answers that are possible before I post, and I also from you learn different ones also ... so my question is ... how do you save your own soul??????

Question:::::now I believe everyone has a path of some kind in this world ... it may not be spiritual but they have one ... I believe that in order to find your spiritual path you must have touched the Higher Power sometime and somewhere in your life ... now maybe the Higher Power showed you something ..or just maybe you got interested in others following a spiritual path ... doesn't matter how you touched base with the Higher Power,,the fact that you did gave you the ability to have a spiritual path if you choose ... now my question is:::::can anyone become spiritual if they truly want to and they touched the Higher Power??????now take into account, being a murderer, or child molester, or done too many bad things on this earth?????

Question:::::now in many cultures the people don't mourn their dead..the religious do with rituals all their own..even some spiritual do also..I choose to be one that really doesn't, but have been teaching my children that if they feel like it, go ahead..it's all about belief and free will isn't it ... now the religious I have found that when someone dies they ask their god why or either say it was divine will, which sort of cuts off their free will ... now the spiritual (some),,,ask their Higher Power or say, it was all in the scheme of things, which again intervenes on free will ... .my question to you is do you think that a god or your Higher Power, has anything to do with when you die??????

comment::::now I have had the opportunity to talk with a whole lot of religious on my groups … usually they message me for whatever reason … they seem to have found that their prayers have been going unanswered … and they want to know why..imagine that..asking a spiritual person that religious question … well all I can tell them is their god of the bible has left the building … due to his malevolent attitude towards his so called people,,, he is no longer in charge of the pe … ople of the world … and this goes for any religion … religious people are leaving their places and not being afraid anymore to question their god … I see more and more each day becoming spiritual … all across the world this is happening..by the thousands..some day the pope will no longer be needed with no followers … I check the numbers as all of you can on the internet … those of you that are religious and still follow the bible is out of fear of retribution if you don't … maybe by being on my groups you will learn something and change … I can only hope because one day we will be the majority ..and maybe this world will be a better place …

Question::::now this comes from my own belief, being spiritual … Karma … we may all look at it differently..but basically it's what goes around, comes around … now if your religious you can go to your church and tell your priest or minister or who ever and they will give you absolution for what it is you feel guilty about … Higher Power knows I have traveled a rough path all my life and have done some things I wish I never did … and I'm sure some of you also are like me … I personally have had to make amends for these things in order to move on and be who I am now … my question is ::::how do you deal with your past indescretions???????

Question:::::now weather you believe your spiritual or religious or an atheist,,,we all have to go through life with what we have … some have gifts, most don't..but what is important is that whatever you chose,,and I do mean chose, not brainwashed into it,,,we all have our battles with our own demons … .some are so fanatical about their beliefs they would anything to promote them..as a spiritual person myself I never let my beliefs take me down that road of fanaticism … and most of us don't … my question is:::how do you deal with someone who is am fanatic???one example is a jehova witness who will damn near knock down your door to tell you about the 10 levels of heaven

_____
_____
_____
_____
_____
_____
_____
_____
_____
_____
_____
_____
_____
_____
_____
_____
_____
_____
_____
_____
_____
_____
_____
_____
_____
_____
_____

Question:::::now I have been reading and watching vids about this old thing called law of attraction.. it's been around for thousands of yrs but probably called by different names … I don't want to know who uses it and if they got what they wanted,,I want to know how many tried it seriously and gotten nothing??????

Question:::::now I have had several comments on my posts regarding witches … I don't know why but some of you who claim to be spiritual think there is something wrong with being a witch … the name has been given a bad rap..and those of you probably know nothing about them or what they do and how they are also spiritual … .I forgive your ignorance..maybe you should learn more about them … maybe you would also attack pagans, gnostics, druids and wiccans also amongst the alread … y wiped out people by the catholic faith … that's a fact and if you don't know, look it up … I personally know someone who has been practicing the arts for over 40 yrs and they are not only spiritual but only do good things to help people … I myself use what you would call spells and am a caster … does that make me a witch?????of course there are the dark ones but we need not fear them … they are far and between and most have no power at all … .my question is::::::if you are one whom believes they are bad, do you have the guts to come forward and explain yourself??????

_____

_____

_____

_____

_____

_____

_____

_____

_____

_____

_____

_____

_____

_____

_____

_____

_____

_____

_____

Question:::::Violence and the belief system of spirituality ... ... first I must say that we being spiritual beings have our own specific ways that we deal with things ... I believe witches, wiccans, pagans, gnostics, and druids and all other belief systems that have been destroyed or tried to are spiritual in their own belief systems ... .then there are the rest of us each believing our own system ... but unlike religion we don't have to adhere to a book and follow it word for word ... ... if we did where would our free will be???? ... I am one who believes that sometimes when appropriate we need to use violence to protect our selves and our belief system ... I know a lot of you don't..but that's OK because we need all kinds of spiritual people as a whole with there basic beliefs, such as being loving, kind, considerate and compassion ... amongst other basic things ... what my question is if you believe in my post give me an AMEN, and if you don't,, please explain why ... thanks

_____
_____
_____
_____
_____
_____
_____
_____
_____
_____
_____
_____
_____
_____
_____
_____
_____
_____
_____
_____
_____
_____
_____

Question:::::now when talking with a religious person and they use the word god,, I always ask them is it the god of the bible … this is because some people don't follow the god of the bible but say they are religious and spiritual at the same time … the ones who say it is the god of the bible are accepting everything their god has done in both testaments … my question is:::::how can anyone believe in the god of the old testament and still accept that religion,,and say they are spiritual at the same time????????

Question:::::now there comes a time when you are working on being a spiritual being ... In the beginning of your journey or path ... you want to learn and practice all you can to achieve this goal ... others who believe themselves to be spiritual will tell you to do things in a certain way to get to that point of finally crossing over the line into being spiritual ... before you do you might have been religious or followed another belief system ... my question is::::what happened to set you on the path of spiritualism?????

Question:::::now I won't mince words as they say and just tell it the way I see it before my question … .being spiritual of course you want to help others … but the first time you get screwed, yes I said it that's what I call it,,,the second time I call it really screwed..and the third time is a charm, and that's called Royaly Screwed … lolol … of course it doesn't have to be with the same person … even being spiritual you can't go through life getting screwed over by everyon … e you try to help … herein lies Judgement..but that's not what I want to ask … .I want to talk about forgiveness and forget … all of you I'm sure want to be spiritual and forgive for WHATEVER reason … let's not discuss that here and now … .but what about forgetting and putting things in the past … my question to you is:::::how many times do you think you shouldn't judge and get royaly screwed and should you just forget and move on?????and please don't take offence at my words, that's not the point here …

_____
_____
_____
_____
_____
_____
_____
_____
_____
_____
_____
_____
_____
_____
_____
_____
_____
_____
_____
_____
_____
_____
_____
_____

question::::a little while ago my 12 yr old and I were in the kitchen … he was supposed to take his cough medicine, and was trying to change subjects thinking I would forget.lolol … we were joking around and I told him I wasn't so stupid for him to try and do that and if he didn't take it I would bring down upon him the wrath of Satan himself … he started laughing and then I did because, as a spiritual person as was his mom, we taught him there is no satan … he believes in a … ngels and demons and light and dark … and he knows are home is protected from the darkness … he is gifted and has been seeing things for about the last few yrs … which we explain to him depending on what he sees … anyway I told him I would post this and ask a question … he can't wait to see … so my question is::::::do any of you out there have children who the situation is similar to??????

Question::::now for those of you following my posts lately, you might have noticed that I have been talking about religion and spirituality in the same post ... I am spiritual, but I have nothing against anyone who is religious ... I am just looking for possible similarities or difference..now if you are religious you might bow down and kiss the ring of the pope if you ever met him..I personally would not ... but I would show the same amount of respect that he would show me.this I would do for anyone in a position of authority that would be considered over me ... now my question is :::if you don't believe in religion, what would you do if you met the pope????????

Question:::::::::well we talked about empaths and healers, now let's talk about having NO gifts … to be spiritual we don't have to have any gifts whatsoever … we have no books as the bible or Koran, or etc to tell us what to do or how to act((((thank the Higher Power))) … lololo … but some people act spiritual without ever thinking about being spiritual … .they love all, have compassion for all, are alighned with nature,, and you know the rest … .if you told them they were acting in the belief of being spiritual, they might look at you and not even understand … .they have no gifts … my question to you is ::::::are you one of these people who started this way before finding your path??????

_____

_____

_____

_____

_____

_____

_____

_____

_____

_____

_____

_____

_____

_____

_____

_____

_____

_____

_____

_____

_____

_____

_____

_____

_____

_____

_____

question::::now I read here a lot on spiritual awakening … some even ask how to do it..well we know it's different for everyone and some never do … but I believe it's also a different kind of awakening for everyone..no 2 people have the same one..that's what's great about it … being individual but part of the whole..now my question to you is:::::what was your individual awakening if you have had it yet?????

_____

_____

_____

_____

_____

_____

_____

_____

_____

_____

_____

_____

_____

_____

_____

_____

_____

_____

_____

_____

_____

_____

_____

_____

_____

_____

question::::now I read here a lot on spiritual awakening … some even ask how to do it..well we know it's different for everyone and some never do … but I believe it's also a different kind of awakening for everyone..no 2 people have the same one..that's what's great about it … being individual but part of the whole..now my question to you is:::::what was your individual awakening if you have had it yet?????

---

question:::::the Higher Power, is what some would call the alpha and the omega ... no beginning and no end ... but that's just too much for our minds to comprehend ... .let's just call it the top dog ... lol ... I believe there at one time was a god that the Higher Power put here to deal with us humans ... .but it wasn't perfect and fell to a place where it wanted ALL humans to just obey it ... the bible tells us the story as written by those who witnessed it ... it became a malevolent ... god and in time was taken away by the Higher Power ... .and the Higher Power decided to do the job itself for a time ... when it left it left us with the knowledge of it's existence ... and that's why people now are becoming spiritual ... it's always here when and if we need it ... but that comes with TRUE BELIEF, of it's existence ... ... .ALL your religious books can now be thrown aside and ignored what happened back then ... take a deep breath and think about what I just said ... no more having to live like a slave to a god ... no more hell ... only learning ... and advancing in knowledge ... mistakes will always be made but without the consequences that is in the bible ... ... .my question to you is;;;;;;;;do you want this spiritual life or go back to your malevolent god who no longer exists and continue to punish yourselves??????

_____
_____
_____
_____
_____
_____
_____
_____
_____
_____
_____
_____
_____
_____
_____
_____
_____
_____
_____

Question:::::so there were these 2 families living very close to each other and so they were thought to be friends by everyone around … one day the father of one family stole something from the other family … when it was found out the father from whom it was stolen asked to talk to the father who stole from him … he told him he knew of the theft and the other apologized and said he needed to make some money for food … the first said, why did you not come to me and ask..the … second said he was too embarrassed..well the first forgave him and they went on their way … now down the road the first family had all sorts of parties and things happening in the neighborhood but never was the thief ever invited … one day he asked why since he had forgiven him was he not back in the others good graces … .did he not think he was punished enough for his misdeed … the other said I am not punishing you ..you see the forgiveness has nothing to do with you coming to my parties ..the fact is I cannot trust you anymore and therefore I banished you from all that we do … MY Question is what would you have done in this situation??????

_____
_____
_____
_____
_____
_____
_____
_____
_____
_____
_____
_____
_____
_____
_____
_____
_____
_____
_____
_____
_____
_____

Jesus, was just a man. No son of god..but he was spiritual.that's the only reason I like him … many other people in life that are great were spiritual but they couldn't sway the masses … but we keep trying

Question:::::being spiritual means many different things to many different people ... they practice different things and believe different things ... some feel spiritual when they take a walk in the woods ... some when they help others ... some when they talk to their angels or spirits or their Higher Power ... the list could go on forever..and we talked about the basics before ... sometimes the darkest is when one is trying to act spiritual because, as we know the dark, hates that ... my question is:::::::how many of you have been attacked by the dark while trying to do something spiritual??????

_____
_____
_____
_____
_____
_____
_____
_____
_____
_____
_____
_____
_____
_____
_____
_____
_____
_____
_____
_____
_____
_____
_____
_____

Question::::duality, the whole vs. the individual … .the greatest thing about being spiritual and not religious, is that we don't have to be sheeple led to the slaughter..we don't have a book that tells us what to do and what not to do … we don't ALL have to believe exactly the same thing … we can be an individual with some different ideas and still be all spiritual, and part of the whole … let me tell you how I can explain it … take a car for instance and say it's the whole … take you, and say your the alternater … you are an individual part of the whole … very simple to understand … is it not … so there's your duality … now my question to you is:::::::do you still say there is no individual, and only the whole,,,and explain your idea??????

Question::::I think I'll call this comment/question,,,forward or fall … Now I don't care who says they know it all, or if people think their personal spiritual teachers, know it all also … their are plenty of people who claim to be prophets out there who claim to be jesus reincarnate … I personally think jesus was just a man..gifted yes but just a man … had some great ideas that still help mankind along their paths … .but I'm sure that jesus himself, no son of any god, would tell you he learned new things every day … same goes for Bhudda … only a gifted man who learned things every day … I myself would never claim to know it all when I learn new things from all of you every day as I try to teach things I have learned back to you … my question is::::have you ever met someone who claims to know it all?????

_____
_____
_____
_____
_____
_____
_____
_____
_____
_____
_____
_____
_____
_____
_____
_____
_____
_____
_____
_____
_____
_____
_____

question:::::now, the question of life after death has been around since the beginning of mankind … people along the way have all tried to prove it, including science … not counting death experiences, where people say they followed a light or other explanations … what proof do we have to prove it … it is only faith and belief we have never been proven..this is why we have to have the ultimate faith and belief … we have all seen miracles and helped us believe in supernatural things..but if it never happened to you, then what then … My question is,, what makes you believe in life after mortal death??????

Question:::::now we know for a fact that more people are born then die every day … that's why the population of the world is still growing … now some people believe in reincarnation..so for the sake of a spiritual disagreement, lets say that it's true and say these people who die return to occupy a new birth … but what about all the new bodies … my question is::::with the booming population, where do all the new souls come from????????

Question:::sugar or sweet and low … many people have different ideas about what it is to be spiritual … .we all agree though (I believe) that the bottom line is love, peace, kindness, compassion and all the other things that you would put in that list … but there that claim to be spiritual that for whatever reason don't follow some of those things … I don't know why..maybe their not as far along as would be liked to be … I myself is guilty of breaking a rule now and then when the darkness pushes me too far … but I never hurt anyone … my question is::::telling the truth as someone spiritual have you ever been in that position before you REALLY decided to follow the basics of being spiritual?????don't forget, truth is one of them on the list.lolol

Question:::::now I have religious and spiritual on my groups..but,,the religious say they are spiritual …
I have always said you can't be both at the same time..but hey, if they feel what it is to be both, then
let them..my question has nothing to do with except what they believe..now if your religious and the
spiritual can chime in also … my question is:::::why are there 2 parts to the bible..the old and the
new..first an eye for an eye and the new, turn the other cheek …???????

Question:::::first off NDE's, or what is called near death experience, is not what you think it is ... the name does not mean what you think it is. I had a experience when I was in surgery for my busted appendix ... I had a NDE ... people who say they died and come back did not have a NDE ... this is because they actually died and were brought back ... they had a death experience ... not near death ... so unless you came close to death but didn't die, you didn't have a NDE.my question to you is,,who really had a Death experience??????

It's a good thing I as being spiritual have conditioned my self to not hate ... there are a few die hard religious people on my groups that just don't belong here..they refuse to accept common sence and remain brain washed in their beliefs..I accept certain things from the bible that are positive ..but those who follow the old testament is not one of them.lolo how could anyone in their right mind follow a god that murders his own children,,,no matter why,, ... a malevolent being ... that cares more about itself then his children ... come on people, read the bible, the old testament..and you want to follow a god who changes it's mind and decides to be a nice guy, as in the new testament ... when is the next time it will change its mind and all things change again?????If you follow the whole bible which you have to if religious then you are brainwashed and I hope you see the light before it's too late ...

Question::right to the point..do you believe you can be both religious and spiritual at the same time ... and when I say religious I mean following the bible or any other book that tells you what you should do??????

question::::now this may be quite long.lolol … … there was a farmer who lived on their farm with a wife and 2 kids … it was a family farm handed down to him from his father … it was a medium sized farm about 20 acres … and on it grew all types of fruit plants..and he cultivated all manor of vegetables also,,,he also was a great hunter and fisherman and had a lot of livestock of all kinds … so they never were at a problem with food or shelter … and he never wanted to get ri … ch but have a cozy loving family which he had … he would sell or trade his wares, at the market … and always have enough left over … he was all set for winter which where he lived was a state that never really gets to freezing so he had no problems there with his animals … you get my idea so far I hope … now one day while working in the fields he had a thought that came rushing to his head … why not take all the extras and set up a street sales market … but with no reason why … now they were not perticurily a religious family as his father either … they went to no churches or anything but every mealtime the father would have everyone bow down their heads and thank the Higher Power for what they had … they did no praying of anykind in the house … but it was not a rule … so one day he set up his market next to the street in front of his farm and sold his wares … but he noticed that there were a lot of people with children who passed that looked as if they reall could not afford to buy … the children would come up and look but had no money..so he thought why not give the children some … and the word spread and all the hungry children would come to get some of his wares … he did sell or trade some also … but at the end of the day he felt he had helped others instead of just his family..and every yr his yield to the farm became greater and greater … now as a spiritual person I want you to figure out a morale to the story … and don't be so quick to think you know the answer????????

_____
_____
_____
_____
_____
_____
_____
_____
_____
_____
_____
_____
_____

Question::::for both those searching and already on their path … their will come a time in which you will have to make a decision … from the crossroads you will have a choice to change direction or stay the course … and for those searching which way also … now we all know we have free will … their might be signs..some dark and some light..but they may not appear that way … no easy decision … so I ask you,,how will you be able to tell the difference between the dark and the light signs???????

Question::::If you follow the bible and go to church and give if you can, you would be considered religious … .that's an organized religion your following … when you are spiritual, and have no book to follow, but follow the root core of being spiritual … that I believe to be, belief in a Higher Power, only do good, as spreading love and compassion, and do for others in need whatever you can if you can … without the want of anything in return..could in any way that be considered an organized belief system which would make it a religion??????

_____
_____
_____
_____
_____
_____
_____
_____
_____
_____
_____
_____
_____
_____
_____
_____
_____
_____
_____
_____
_____
_____
_____
_____
_____
_____
_____
_____

Question:::::being spiritual … well I believe all the prophets as Buddah, Christ, and the Dali Lama, along with so many more, were all spiritual and not religious … there has never been a leader of men that was so wise that they followed or taught religion … now my question is:::::what is it that can make a person spiritual????????

comment:::::since so many people seem not to understand my post about the fisherman, I will say this … too many people who claim to be spiritual think all they have to do is help and their job is done and over … sorry, it's not … we are responsible for anything that happens because of our choices or actions, with anyone … … whether it be simple or complicated … example..your walking down the street and a beggar is on the corner..you want to give him some money..but as you ap … proach you notice the stench of alchohol coming off him … .if you give him the money and say, well I helped, and he buys a bottle with it and walks out drunk in front of the bus and gets killed … is it not part of your fault … don't even bother trying to talk your way out of the situation to make yourself not guilty … … this is how I'm finding more and more spiritual people acting … not ever responsible for their choices and actions … well you don't have to comment. You know who you are … spend your time trying to squeeze yourself into a righteous place … goodnite and may your Higher Power go with you and yours>>>>>

Question:::::question and comments ... sometimes I post comments ..but if you notice I never say anything like this is the TRUTH ... .that's because everyone has their own truth until they meet someone with a similar truth ... I always say, this is what I believe ... .but for my questions, one of the reasons I post them is to see other spiritual answers so I can grow my personal knowledge and expand and strengthen my path with your answers that are not mine ... I always have a personal answer to my questions ... remember I said one of my reasons???my question is what do you think the main reason I have for posting my questions????????

Question::::now there are many belief systems that existed long before the catholics were around … some include the Pagans, Gnostics, Druids., and let's not forget witches..and much was stolen by the catholics and made them their own … but that's all past now … and I believe they are considered spiritual if you were to give an overall label … my question to you is, does your spirituality have any ties to the old world of belief systems??????

_____
_____
_____
_____
_____
_____
_____
_____
_____
_____
_____
_____
_____
_____
_____
_____
_____
_____
_____
_____
_____
_____
_____
_____
_____
_____
_____

Question:::::now I won't mince words as they say and just tell it the way I see it before my question … .being spiritual of course you want to help others … but the first time you get screwed, yes I said it that's what I call it,,,the second time I call it really screwed..and the third time is a charm, and that's called Royaly Screwed … lolol … of course it doesn't have to be with the same person … even being spiritual you can't go through life getting screwed over by everyon … e you try to help … herein lies Judgement..but that's not what I want to ask … .I want to talk about forgiveness and forget … all of you I'm sure want to be spiritual and forgive for WHATEVER reason … let's not discuss that here and now … .but what about forgetting and putting things in the past … my question to you is:::::how many times do you think you shouldn't judge and get royaly screwed and should you just forget and move on?????and please don't take offence at my words, that's not the point here …

_____
_____
_____
_____
_____
_____
_____
_____
_____
_____
_____
_____
_____
_____
_____
_____
_____
_____
_____
_____

question:::::::now I believe the beginning of spiritual started back in the 60's with free love and peace and non violence ... but that went all to hell didn't it ... and now a few are trying to bring it back ... not a chance any more ... too many people are dark and evil and self serving and they love it that way ... they will learn their ways were bad, but not in my time ... I will be long gone if the world ever changes to be a spiritual place ... all I see around me is hate and ignorance and destruction ... way too much to change now ... so I ask you, what do you think your faith being spiritual do besides helping your self????????

question::::well most of you who comment here to my posts understand me and who I am … I claim not to be a know it all but I do have decades of knowledge and experience, behind me … .I have studied old belief systems and studied under people who kept the old … I could never have learned everything, because I am only human and have a human mind … but I learned enough to know when someone is a bullshitter.lolol … I have these spiritual groups to help people grow and understa … nd what it is to be spiritual … .and to help them along their path, if needed … if at any time anyone wants to confront me, I will be more then happy to do that, right here and now … my faith is stronger then you can imagine … don't follow me, just follow yourself … that's why I ask the questions..to get you to open your mind and explore your spirituality … I wish you all well on your journeys question::::now the level of spirituality is dependent on your lifestyle … people think all you have to do is have unconditional love and empathy and all the simple traits that a spiritual person should have … yes you may be spiritual but only at the bottom … there are degrees also that matter..the higher the degree the more that person will be seeking more answers to questions … .but I'm sorry to say most are happy right there on the bottom, being basic spirituality … … of course this is only my opinion, but if you think about it, it will make sence and maybe you will spend more time moving forward and upward … my question is::::::do you think that there are different levels of being spiritual and how do you get there??????

Question:::::lets go outside the box that doesn't really exist for a moment … I believe we were seeded here by the Higher Power … maybe through a higher race then us but by his will … and many different seeds were planted and that's why we have such a vast amount of different people … now I don't believe in the theory that we grew from any other species … my opinion … that would to me explain a lot right now … and why the world is the way it is now … .my question is::::where do you think our ancestors came from and why??????

_____

_____

_____

_____

_____

_____

_____

_____

_____

_____

_____

_____

_____

_____

_____

_____

_____

_____

_____

_____

_____

_____

_____

_____

Question:::::witches and spellcasting … now my wife was a pagan but also a spellcaster for about 40 yrs … I myself am simply spiritual but at times have been a spellcaster … the catholic church does rituals every day but nobody calls them witches..their are good and bad spellcasters all around but can also be something else also … most try to keep themselves hidden in the shadows because of what people tend to do to them and that is put negative judgement upon them … regardless of what they practice … just like the past as it is today … now my question to you if you wish to answer is:::::what is your opinion about them???????

_____

_____

_____

_____

_____

_____

_____

_____

_____

_____

_____

_____

_____

_____

_____

_____

_____

_____

_____

_____

_____

_____

_____

_____

Question::::well we know that all people are individuals … but when it comes to being spiritual we also say we must have our own paths … sometimes our paths cross but only for a moment before we go on our separate ways because of some different thing we believe to be true … .being spiritual is doing and believing in and doing all the Right things and none of the wrong as religion does … come on now the holy crusades..and wars now based on religions … can't deny any of it … but that's not ever going to bring ALL people together … wouldn't it be awesome to have the whole world living under an umbrella of being spiritual.my question to you is::::how can this occur and what do we need to do it???????

_____
_____
_____
_____
_____
_____
_____
_____
_____
_____
_____
_____
_____
_____
_____
_____
_____
_____
_____
_____
_____
_____

Question:::::well I did empath so now I would like to do healers ... well as you all know there are many different kinds ... but would it surprise you if you knew that a lot of people who now and have went to Medical school believe they had a calling ... something spiritual that told them that's what they needed or felt they had to do and are not athiests ... they even believe in the miracles of spiritual healings along with medical science ... .well it's true.look it up ... I am ge ... tting older now and my abilities to heal are losing their power ... I don't do the healing anyway and never had ... the Higher Power always provided that. I was just a conduit ... but my levels of power are diminishing with age ... so now I prefer to teach what I know and have learned over the years ... ... and I have a different way as you all know ... so, my question to you is::::::are you a healer that's new, or old and have the belief strong enough to do it until you can't anymore???????

_____

_____

_____

_____

_____

_____

_____

_____

_____

_____

_____

_____

_____

_____

_____

_____

_____

_____

_____

_____

_____

_____

_____

Question:::::now bear with me until I get to my question.lol … the pentagram, 5 pointed star..anyone spiritual should know what it means … the 5 points are for the elementals … fire, water, air and earth … the fifth one representing your life force or soul or spirit … but, the point has to always be pointing up which is north..the same as if you were to paint it on the ground … a point must face north … .now I have several of them..when I go out I like to wear one where people … can see … sometimes they will ask me about it and then the conversation begins … now the catholics and Christians have a symbol also..the cross..funny thing is if they where it upside down people will think them evil … the truth is the POPE himself has a chair with a upside down cross on it … look it up and see what it means in there religion..you will be surprised … now my question to you is::::do you wear outside your clothes any religious or spiritual symbol where people can see it????????

question:::::well just remember my comments and my questions are all coming from my talks with MY Higher Power … yes I said mine, because there are many other lower gods and goddesses out there still with their own agendas … figure it out … now people say that after they die they make a deal to come back for a reason … bullshit.would you choose to come back to die of disease, or die as a child, or etc … of course not … you may however decide to come back to accomplish something … you didn't before … but don't forget you have free will … so while your on your journey to accomplish this thing that your sub-conscience only knows when you have talks with your Higher Power in you sleep and work out new deals all the time … seem to complicated, no, real simple … you ever wonder why you don't always get what you want but what you need … that's why you will eventually get what you came back down for but when it's the right time … of course this only happens to TRUE BELIEVERS … the rest are on their own … It only takes 1 to change a world … and that's while in a conscience state we remember nothing … so my question to you is::::::is this statement possible, and what do you THINK of the idea????????now it's time to open your minds a little more … .

_____

_____

_____

_____

_____

_____

_____

_____

_____

_____

_____

_____

_____

_____

_____

_____

_____

_____

_____

_____

_____

_____

Question:::::last for the night.lol aren't you happy.lolol … .I truly have to admire all living things beneath the waters and above, that the Higher Power has created … except us … they all have a direct connection to the Higher Power, and free will but don't have to learn it as we do … they all live in a sort of harmony, even if it means that they do what is needed to survive … .but us, we have all these other tendencies other then peace … greed, lust, having to be dominant over everything else … you get the idea I hope … .so my question to you is:::::why weren't we created as everything else and can live in perfect harmony as they do??????

Question::: Truth,,,A truth, or The TRUTH..of course everyone has some one, maybe a whole lot … the video and the books about the Secret and the Law of Attraction, claim to tell you the Truth … pick up any spiritual book and read it and by the end it will let you know what the Truth is..at least that's what they will claim … now of course as usual these are only my thoughts and beliefs on the subject … out of 8 billion people on this rock your chances of getting something thr … ough a books truth or the Secret are about as good as getting killed in a plane crash if you flew a thousand times … why you ask..well maybe it's not THE TRUTH … now those of you who have been around with me for awhile have see some small miracles performed through belief ..and that my friends is the Real Secret of the Real TRUTH … the highest truth there is or will ever believe..BELIEF, REAL BELIEF, NOT just going through the motions of being spiritual … I have had people message me and asked,,I do everything I can to be spiritual but never get any help … what's the problem … and I tell them, it's not what you do but what you believe, and I guess you don't REALLY believe … then they get mad and go away … lolol … so I say to you the FIRST, BASIC, and MOST POWERFULL TRUTH IS YOUR BELIEF IN YOUR Higher Power … .so my question to you is what do you think is your most powerfull truth??????

_____
_____
_____
_____
_____
_____
_____
_____
_____
_____
_____
_____
_____
_____
_____
_____
_____
_____
_____

Question::::empaths, a rare breed … to have this gift can be a blessing or a curse … I know, I'm one … now some people don't have to be empaths to be able to read people … they can do it normally if for some reason they learned the tricks to reading body language and speech patterns … and some people like myself can do both ..now my gift was once a curse..because sometimes when I went to places like a funeral I would get too many messages and my emotions could not control t … hem … which you can imagine the shit that it would make my mind go through … .add to that the act of compassion and it can be a real mess … but over the yrs I have honed my gift to be a blessing.and I know now how to control it and shut out what I don't want coming in … so my question is ::::if you are an empath whether knew to it or an old timer like me … what do you think about what you are or have went through??????

_____
_____
_____
_____
_____
_____
_____
_____
_____
_____
_____
_____
_____
_____
_____
_____
_____
_____
_____
_____
_____
_____

Question:::::I believe,,I know … 2 different statements..meaning 2 absolutely different things … when you say you believe that means you have no proof, but you believe it to be possible … when you say you Know that means you have gotten proof of something … sometimes I interchange them … but in reality they do mean 2 different things … when I speak of a Higher Power, I know it exists because I have seen proof … I love it when someone says that they believe in Jesus for instan … ce … they have no REAL proof of his existence or powers except that which they have read in a book, usually the bible … now I'm not here to dismiss peoples belief in Jesus … was just making a point … also take Angels,, if you have ever seen one then you Know, you don't have to believe … but if you haven't you probably believe in them … I hope you see how the 2 are very different … my question is:::::when we speak of a Higher Power, or if you want to call it god or source or universe or whatever,,,do you believe in it or do you Know?????

_____
_____
_____
_____
_____
_____
_____
_____
_____
_____
_____
_____
_____
_____
_____
_____
_____
_____
_____
_____
_____
_____

Comment:::::::to everyone … I have talked with many of you who have been in a position of your belief where NO ONE has backed you or believed in you … .you have told me how much you have felt all alone and condemned by what you believe..well let me tell you something … you are not alone..people who would love to be spiritual are too afraid of their brainwashing to deny their god … .it takes a lot of belief to become spiritual … we have no books to follow.or rules as the reli … gious do … I used to be religious but I made it out with a lot of belief and faith that what I was doing was right … you could say I saw the LIGHT … .now, I don't give a shit what anybody says about me … I wear my pentagram … and the ignorant are only scared … if you know what the pentagram means then you know it's not evil … .I'm old now, and I really am tired of fighting off all the darkness in this world … you, the younger generation, are to fulfill the faith and belief of the spiritual if you really want a better world … I can only guide now. My fighting days are gone … I hope for the sake of the Higher Power..you will prevail … .and may your Higher Power go with you … …

Question:::::now I have heard people say and have written here there is no such thing as the devil … and they are ALL right … but there is a force of darkness and evil that is around us every day … some people believe they are above that and can't be attacked or harmed … well I hope your ready if it ever happens … it probably won't though … because there is a saying that goes like this … the greatest harm the devil ever did to mankind is make them believe that he doesn't exist … lolol … but that refers to the evil and darkness and no devil … so the next time you think your beyond reproach … think again … my question is:::::has anyone ever thought they were beyond being messed with by the darkness, but learned a very valuable lesson????????

Question:::::now I know many of you say not to judge and I have explained my reasons for doing it ... this will never change because it sometimes helps to stop evil or darkness before it comes ... and as far as those who say get rid of your ego,,,we all need one to survive or we never will move forward..but it does need to be controlled ... my questions were always meant to get people to think and expand their minds with other possibilities ... for some this has worked ... and I'm grateful for that ... for some it does nothing and for that I feel sorrow ... being spiritual for me not only means doing the basics, but to go a step forward at every chance ... without the forward movement we will only become stagnate and die spiritually ... .my question is::::what have you done lately to move forward and learn something new????????

Questionn-empaths, a rare breed … to have this gift can be a blessing or a curse … I know, I'm one … now some people don't have to be empaths to be able to read people … they can do it normally if for some reason they learned the tricks to reading body language and speech patterns … and some people like myself can do both ..now my gift was once a curse..because sometimes when I went to places like a funeral I would get too many messages and my emotions could not control t … hem … which you can imagine the shit that it would make my mind go through … .add to that the act of compassion and it can be a real mess … but over the yrs I have honed my gift to be a blessing.and I know now how to control it and shut out what I don't want coming in … so my question is ::::if you are an empath whether knew to it or an old timer like me … what do you think about what you are or have went through??????

_____

_____

_____

_____

_____

_____

_____

_____

_____

_____

_____

_____

_____

_____

_____

_____

_____

_____

_____

_____

_____

_____

_____

_____

_____

_____

question:::::have you ever been soooo depressed for any reason and it hits you like a brick in the face … .you can't figure out why … and so you want to react in a certain way to get rid of the pain it causes … … but then for a moment you think about yourself and being spiritual and look for a way out without hurting yourself or anyone else … … think about the question before you jump to an answer.my question;;;;;;;is what would you do or what have you done to deal with the situation??????????

Question::::::::well we talked about empaths and healers, now let's talk about having NO gifts … to be spiritual we don't have to have any gifts whatsoever … we have no books as the bible or Koran, or etc to tell us what to do or how to act(((((thank the Higher Power))) … lololo … but some people act spiritual without ever thinking about being spiritual … .they love all, have compassion for all, are alighned with nature,, and you know the rest … .if you told them they were acting in the belief of being spiritual, they might look at you and not even understand … .they have no gifts … my question to you is :::::::are you one of these people who started this way before finding your path??????

_____

_____

_____

_____

_____

_____

_____

_____

_____

_____

_____

_____

_____

_____

_____

_____

_____

_____

_____

_____

_____

_____

_____

_____

_____

question:::now if you claim to be spiritual then you know all the basics … everything based around love and compassion … .and some even know that it's not always cut and dry when it comes to that and we may need to battle … .that's why we have ones who are warriors … to pick up the slack and protect the rest of you … now if you don't believe in that then you don't know being spiritual as well as you think … it's been like this for ages … .so my question to you is:::::do you believe in spiritual Warriors to do what I said?????

question:::::I have watched people comment on my questions ... very few considering the amount of people posting ... they seem not to care nor take the time to comment even though being spiritual (as they think they are by their posts)they believe these questions pose no interest to them ... but wait till the first time something on one of the subjects effects them and their begging for help ... lolol ... then they will wish they paid more attention ... lolol ... anyway my question is::::has anything ever happened to you that you have some knowledge of because you were interested and commented on those posts???????

Question:::::now it is my personal opinion that those who claim to be witches, have a long line of heritage that dates back centuries as do the other spiritual peoples as the pagans and gnostics and the druids and more … for the most part they are spiritual and good.but because of things that happened in times ago they have been given a bad name … … but most of you are afraid still to see their light and so you make them hide.when they can be of great strength in communion with the spiritual of today … my wife was one who ran her own covent at one time until she decided to become a solitary … I still keep up her alter … my question is :::::why do you spiritual always say you don't judge but do it every day to people like them???????

Question:::::now it is my personal opinion that those who claim to be witches, have a long line of heritage that dates back centuries as do the other spiritual peoples as the pagans and gnostics and the druids and more … for the most part they are spiritual and good.but because of things that happened in times ago they have been given a bad name … … but most of you are afraid still to see their light and so you make them hide.when they can be of great strength in communion with the spiritual of today … my wife was one who ran her own covent at one time until she decided to become a solitary … I still keep up her alter … my question is :::::why do you spiritual always say you don't judge but do it every day to people like them???????

Question:::::::now as earlier I posted, I was just sitting in the kitchen, thinking really about nothing and then a question to ask came to me … .when we pass on and become one with our Higher Power, even though we are still that individual soul,,,do we bring with us any yearnings for anything we liked in this world … not the question though … what if we loved to eat a certain kind of ice cream every night … could we, as I believe. Come down in a physical form and go to a place we had it and have it again … .just pop in and have it and leave … and as payment, leave a note that says I owe you, when you are in need just call me and I will come and help you … … my question to you is it possible to do something like this???????

Question:::::::now as earlier I posted, I was just sitting in the kitchen, thinking really about nothing and then a question to ask came to me … .when we pass on and become one with our Higher Power, even though we are still that individual soul,,,do we bring with us any yearnings for anything we liked in this world … not the question though … what if we loved to eat a certain kind of ice cream every night … could we, as I believe. Come down in a physical form and go to a place we had it and have it again … .just pop in and have it and leave … and as payment, leave a note that says I owe you, when you are in need just call me and I will come and help you … … my question to you is it possible to do something like this???????

question:::::now the level of spirituality is dependent on your lifestyle ... people think all you have to do is have unconditional love and empathy and all the simple traits that a spiritual person should have ... yes you may be spiritual but only at the bottom ... there are degrees also that matter..the higher the degree the more that person will be seeking more answers to questions ... .but I'm sorry to say most are happy right there on the bottom, being basic spirituality ... ... of course this is only my opinion, but if you think about it, it will make sence and maybe you will spend more time moving forward and upward ... my question is::::::do you think that there are different levels of being spiritual and how do you get there??????

question for today:::::::now many people have many different gifts … some more then one … and some none at all … some are learning them and some are afraid of them..my question to you is:::::what do you believe to be the most powerful gift one can have???????

Question:::::now I know that most of you realize why I ask my   , it's not to just get answers because I'm a dumb ass..lolol … .it's to help you spiritual people open your minds, as I do before asking the question … I will get a thought or question from the Higher Power and then ponder the possible answers … sometimes I spend 20 minutes before I get an answer that makes sence to me … and it may not even be the truth..and that's a whole other subject.lolol … .but after I ask I see your answers and sometimes learn something new about what I asked … because I keep my mind open to all possibilities … so it is a learning situation for all … now my question to you is:::::what do you think is more effective,,,reading a book where they want you to believe what they have written or the questions that I ask and why?????

_____

_____

_____

_____

_____

_____

_____

_____

_____

_____

_____

_____

_____

_____

_____

_____

_____

_____

_____

_____

_____

_____

_____

Question:::::now this morning my 12 yr old son mike and I were talking about his dreams ... but somehow we got on the subject of shadow people ... for the last few yrs my son has been experiencing supernatural things ... once he saw a lady and child, little girl,,all dressed up in very old clothing from another era..standing in my kitchen and then someone or thing came out my bedroom door and all disappeared..he has also been in the kitchen making breakfast and he heard in one of hi ... s ears the word Zozo, with a woosh of air in his ear,,,,,I told him to look up the name and it said evil spirit or demon ... I told him if he heard it again just laugh because it can't hurt you, just try to scare you ... and then there are the shadow people which he has only seen through the corner of his eyes and when he looked they were gone ... I told them they don't like to be seen ... I once saw one for a few moment in whole ... I was in my kitchen having coffee and all the way in the living room one appeared and started slowly looking around..it had its back to me so I saw it, but then it turned and saw me and disappeared into the front hall way ... ... anyway I told him to look it up and he came up with two different answers for what they are ... one said evil spirits and the other said entities that can scare the shit out of you but are harmless..now I keep reassuring mike we can not have evil in the house because of the cleansing and rituals I do on my wifes alter ... but my question to you is:::::what do you think about shadow people????????

last one for today dear.lolol

_____
_____
_____
_____
_____
_____
_____
_____
_____
_____
_____
_____

question:::::now my dream has been always to live in a community of spiritual people ... living independently from the world around us ... that's not to say we could not be friends with people nearby and maybe even trade with them ... like some of the movies, but without the mistakes they made..lol ... we might be even called a commune, but we would never show ourselves to be any cult in any way ... the Mormons do it!!!! Well I don't think I'll live to see it, but maybe it will happen someday and grow to be something great ... my question is::::how many out there would be willing to give up everything they have to be a part of it???????

question for today::::::::now many people have many different gifts ... some more then one ... and some none at all ... some are learning them and some are afraid of them..my question to you is:::::what do you believe to be the most powerful gift one can have???????

_____

_____

_____

_____

_____

_____

_____

_____

_____

_____

_____

_____

_____

_____

_____

_____

_____

_____

_____

_____

_____

_____

_____

_____

_____

_____

_____

_____

question:::::well I'm sure most of us were not born spiritual but found our paths or journeys somewhere through our lives ... and I'm sure we all did some things that we wish we didn't do, looking back as being spiritual now ... now we come to Karma ... all of us at some time either had children or relatives which we have done wrong for whatever reason ... and if your truly spiritual you have been trying to make up for it because you believe in Karma ... the ones who don't believe are ... the ones who think if someone forgives them then everything is ok and paid for or just don't believe in karma itself ... just excuses to try and get out of the circle of payback ... .so my question to you is:::::before you became spiritual and maybe even after have you done something evil or dark or bad to some relative or children in which you are now trying to make amends for???????

_____
_____
_____
_____
_____
_____
_____
_____
_____
_____
_____
_____
_____
_____
_____
_____
_____
_____
_____
_____
_____

spell::::ok I have had a few people who have asked me how to cleanse their homes from unwanted spirits or darkness … I will post it here … first you need to get ingrediants … about a quarter pound of salt depending on your house or apartment size,,,,1 white candle … 1 smudge stick … .4 green glass bottles … now you must do the ritual EXACTLY as explained or it won't work … first you must start at the top of your house and in every room sprinkle a little salt in EVERY corn … er … do this for ALL rooms and hallways and any attached structures connected to your house or apartment … go to the kitchen and on the table make a circle of salt and put the candle in the middle … fill the 4 glass bottles half way up and put them on the table … … go the highest room you started salting and light the smudge stick until it starts to burn and smoke … now you can use your own terms for the Higher Power if you wish but I use Higher Power … .then repeat as you go through the room and spread the smoke around … In the name of the Higher Power I command all unwanted and unclean spirits to leave … work your way down doing the same thing … the kitchen should be the last room … when you are done with this place the glass bottles at all 4 corners … east, west, south and north.inside the house somewhere … if while your doing this if something happens don't fear, it's only the spirits being pissed off they are being removed … … then blow out the candle and clean up, throw the salt outside your front door … the bottles with the water are to catch any unwanted or unclean spirits from reentering the house … … simple if you follow the directions … old world Pagan spell …

Question:::while I was in the hosp. a few weeks ago for my burst appendix I was in the ICU after surgery … after a few days the chaplain came to visit ..after about 1 sentence I informed him I wasn't religious but spiritual..he seemed stunned as if no one ever said that to him.lol … he then said some neutral stuff about getting better and left … I say thyis because I consider myself spiritual,, but also have an open mind to take in other belief systems sometimes, if they run along side my own … some people don't do that and stick to their one belief … my question is :::which one are you???????

Question:::::you wanna know something about me..I really don't care what people think about what I say or think … I am me and I am a spiritual person … I can forgive all that has ever been done to me and still try to help those people to find their path if they choose … I am old and also wise … and if our Higher Power calls me back tonight,, I will go peacefully, knowing that I have done everything I could while on this rock, to bring people together spiritualy … my question is::::how many of you can say the same?????

Comment::::now that I have put out there the possibility to change vibration and see things not meant for the normal sences ... I will say by a close relationship with your Higher Power, you can see whatever you want without changing anything ... ... just my belief question for today:::::::now many people have many different gifts … some more then one … and some none at all … some are learning them and some are afraid of them..my question to you is:::::what do you believe to be the most powerful gift one can have???????

_____
_____
_____
_____
_____
_____
_____
_____
_____
_____
_____
_____
_____
_____
_____
_____
_____
_____
_____
_____
_____
_____
_____
_____
_____
_____
_____
_____

Question::::::now as earlier I posted, I was just sitting in the kitchen, thinking really about nothing and then a question to ask came to me … .when we pass on and become one with our Higher Power, even though we are still that individual soul,,,do we bring with us any yearnings for anything we liked in this world … not the question though … what if we loved to eat a certain kind of ice cream every night … could we, as I believe. Come down in a physical form and go to a place we had it and have it again … .just pop in and have it and leave … and as payment, leave a note that says I owe you, when you are in need just call me and I will come and help you … … my question to you is it possible to do something like this???????

Question:::::::now as earlier I posted, I was just sitting in the kitchen, thinking really about nothing and then a question to ask came to me … .when we pass on and become one with our Higher Power, even though we are still that individual soul,,,do we bring with us any yearnings for anything we liked in this world … not the question though … what if we loved to eat a certain kind of ice cream every night … could we, as I believe. Come down in a physical form and go to a place we had it and have it again … .just pop in and have it and leave … and as payment, leave a note that says I owe you, when you are in need just call me and I will come and help you … … my question to you is it possible to do something like this???????

Question:::::now it is my personal opinion that those who claim to be witches,have a long line of heritage that dates back centuries as do the other spiritual peoples as the pagans and gnostics and the druids and more ... for the most part they are spiritual and good.but because of things that happened in times ago they have been given a bad name ... .but most of you are afraid still to see their light and so you make them hide.when they can be of great strength in communion with the spiritual of today ... my wife was one who ran her own covent at onetime until she decided to become a solitary ...! still keep up her alter ... my question is :::::why do you spiritual always say you don't judge but do it every day to people like them???????

Question:::::Now I believe that ALL living things have a soul, or spirit, or life force … whatever you want to call it … but I also believe that All living things were born spiritual with the connection to the Higher Power … .we see this in animals all the time..they only do what is necessary to survive … they don't kill for sport and even nurture other types of animals occasionally … beside their own … in the ecosystem of the ocean we see all the time how species coexist need … ing each other to survive … don't ask me why humans fell off that path, and turned to violence for no reason and abuse and taking advantage of each other … but, we are trying to change that back now..and as you know it's no easy task … but my question is:::::do you think the size of a species, as a plant or animal has a different type of soul or spirit or life force then we do, or less or more, or are all our souls equal??????

now many people have many different gifts ... some more then one ... and some none at all ... some are learning them and some are afraid of them..my question to you is:::::what do you believe to be the most powerful gift one can have???????

_____
_____
_____
_____
_____
_____
_____
_____
_____
_____
_____
_____
_____
_____
_____
_____
_____
_____
_____
_____
_____
_____
_____
_____
_____
_____
_____
_____
_____

Comment::::now that I have put out there the possibility to change vibration and see things not meant for the normal sences … I will say by a close relationship with your Higher Power, you can see whatever you want without changing anything … … just my belief

question::::do you ever get the feeling that being spiritual ain't worth a shit … nothing ever works for you no matter how much you talk to your Higher Power … you are sooo close to losing your faith its ridiculous … .you look around and see the haves and the have nots .and wonder why you ain't one of the haves … .but then again you notice that nothing bad ever happens to you ..you never have a battle … you think your special and above all that crap..you think you got it all working for you.. never a problem, so you think your soo spiritual you don't have to fear anything … well yes there are you that are like that and live that life … but my question is:::::what about the rest of us who have to fight every day to uphold our spiritual … what are we???????

question::::do you ever get the feeling that being spiritual ain't worth a shit ... nothing ever works for you no matter how much you talk to your Higher Power ... you are sooo close to losing your faith its ridiculous ... .you look around and see the haves and the have nots .and wonder why you ain't one of the haves ... .but then again you notice that nothing bad ever happens to you ..you never have a battle ... you think your special and above all that crap..you think you got it all working for you.. never a problem, so you think your soo spiritual you don't have to fear anything ... well yes there are you that are like that and live that life ... but my question is:::::what about the rest of us who have to fight every day to uphold our spiritual ... what are we???????

Question:::::::well it appears that many of you believe in science will give you the answers to being spiritual or visa versa ... ... well my simple question to you is::::::::do you go with both or choose one at time??????

Show more reactions

_____
_____
_____
_____
_____
_____
_____
_____
_____
_____
_____
_____
_____
_____
_____
_____
_____
_____
_____
_____
_____
_____
_____
_____

Question:::::now I posed a question on here a little while ago ..it was ... name me one common goal in being spiritual?????? well I had one member not really answer the question directly, but said something about science and spirituality being connected ... .so my question to you now is::::::as much as we know now about science and spirituality,,do you think they are connected at this time as far as we know???????

Question:::::and this is not in any way starting a fight ..I truly would like to hear an answer ... for the religious on the groups, and there are many, but don't ramble on about it ... this question has bothered me for yrs ... no book or priest or reverend has ever been able to answer it ... now there are different types of dark or evil people on this earth..some way nastier then others ... from a simple thief to a mass murderer ... My question is::::when they die and go to hell, how long do they have to be punished depending on their crimes??????you know I don't believe in heaven or hell but am still curious what you think in your beliefs question:::::::since according to one of my recent questions, most believe there can be no mortal Master of spirituality on this earth ..and I hope we all spiritual people strive to have understanding and knowledge while were here. My question is :::::will there come a time before you pass on that you can say your truly happy with your knowledge and ability to help others, or will you go out with something inside you empty?????????

Question:::::so there were these 2 families living very close to each other and so they were thought to be friends by everyone around … one day the father of one family stole something from the other family … when it was found out the father from whom it was stolen asked to talk to the father who stole from him … he told him he knew of the theft and the other apologized and said he needed to make some money for food … the first said, why did you not come to me and ask..the … second said he was too embarrassed..well the first forgave him and they went on their way … now down the road the first family had all sorts of parties and things happening in the neighborhood but never was the thief ever invited … one day he asked why since he had forgiven him was he not back in the others good graces … .did he not think he was punished enough for his misdeed … the other said I am not punishing you ..you see the forgiveness has nothing to do with you coming to my parties ..the fact is I cannot trust you anymore and therefore I banished you from all that we do … MY Question is what would you have done in this situation??????

question::::so who are we … are we religious and follow a bible and a god who destroys his own children … .are we spiritual that when it comes down to battles we run off because we believe not to battle, but to love and think that will win … are we the chosen one who have special powers given to us by the devine to help those in need … are we old world pagans who still use spells to get things done … are we new wave wiccans who basically don't know shit, because they took all their learning from the old ones and don't really know how to use it … are we the ones who can enable us to use our soul force to change things when needed … .my question to you is::::::::you call yourself spiritual, just what are you??????

Question:::::now time comes and it goes … and nothing ever seems to change … why,,because all the spiritual are not united … I have many groups here and I send the same questions to all of them … and what do I get back … all different answers … that's because all spiritual believe they have their own path..their own journey … there really is not a oneness … they say they are all connected to the one, but by their answers, it shows otherwise … .in order to win a battle ALL mus … t follow the same thinking and belief … the spiritual really don't … you all have your own spiritual belief and that's what keeps us apart … all of you reading this, no matter the age, will never live long enough to see the spiritual become the Higher Power on this earth … that's because though we say we are united, we are not really … for yrs I have tried to bring ALL spiritual people together … well it seems I can't … I guess I am just not good enough for what needs to be done … hopefully there will come a time when someone more worthy then I shall succeed … as long as I live I will keep trying, but I fear people just don't want to open their eyes and ears and see and listen … my question is:::::when do you think it will happen?????

_____
_____
_____
_____
_____
_____
_____
_____
_____
_____
_____
_____
_____
_____
_____
_____
_____
_____
_____
_____

Question:::::so there were these 2 families living very close to each other and so they were thought to be friends by everyone around … one day the father of one family stole something from the other family … when it was found out the father from whom it was stolen asked to talk to the father who stole from him … he told him he knew of the theft and the other apologized and said he needed to make some money for food … the first said, why did you not come to me and ask..the … second said he was too embarrassed..well the first forgave him and they went on their way … now down the road the first family had all sorts of parties and things happening in the neighborhood but never was the thief ever invited … one day he asked why since he had forgiven him was he not back in the others good graces … .did he not think he was punished enough for his misdeed … the other said I am not punishing you ..you see the forgiveness has nothing to do with you coming to my parties ..the fact is I cannot trust you anymore and therefore I banished you from all that we do … MY Question is what would you have done in this situation??????

_____
_____
_____
_____
_____
_____
_____
_____
_____
_____
_____
_____
_____
_____
_____
_____
_____
_____
_____
_____
_____

Question:::has anyone out there who is spiritual ever found themselves closer to the animals in mother nature?????

while I was taking a short break from here. ... I was having a short talk with The Higher Power ... .all I can tell you is,, if you are a true believer, then it will leave you with a message ... if you are not and just want to pretend to be,,,,you will be left alone with your life and what you want to believe, and maybe later you will see ... .this is going to happen in a very short time ... so be prepared for something or nothing and that will prove your faith ... when it does happen please post it ...

question:::::well i'm sure most of us were not born spiritual but found our paths or journeys somewhere through our lives … and I'm sure we all did some things that we wish we didn't do, looking back as being spiritual now … now we come to Karma … all of us at some time either had children or relatives which we have done wrong for whatever reason … and if your truly spiritual you have been trying to make up for it because you believe in Karma … the ones who don't believe are … the ones who think if someone forgives them then everything is ok and paid for or just don't believe in karma itself … just excuses to try and get out of the circle of payback … .so my question to you is:::::before you became spiritual and maybe even after have you done something evil or dark or bad to some relative or children in which you are now trying to make amends for???????

spell::::ok I have had a few people who have asked me how to cleanse their homes from unwanted spirits or darkness … I will post it here … first you need to get ingrediants … about a quarter pound of salt depending on your house or apartment size,,,,1 white candle … 1 smudge stick … .4 green glass bottles … now you must do the ritual EXACTLY as explained or it won't work … first you must start at the top of your house and in every room sprinkle a little salt in EVERY corn … er … do this for ALL rooms and hallways and any attached structures connected to your house or apartment … go to the kitchen and on the table make a circle of salt and put the candle in the middle … fill the 4 glass bottles half way up and put them on the table … … go the highest room you started salting and light the smudge stick until it starts to burn and smoke … now you can use your own terms for the Higher Power if you wish but I use Higher Power … .then repeat as you go through the room and spread the smoke around … In the name of the Higher Power I command all unwanted and unclean spirits to leave … work your way down doing the same thing … the kitchen should be the last room … when you are done with this place the glass bottles at all 4 corners … east, west, south and north.inside the house somewhere … if while your doing this if something happens don't fear, it's only the spirits being pissed off they are being removed … … then blow out the candle and clean up, throw the salt outside your front door … the bottles with the water are to catch any unwanted or unclean spirits from reentering the house … … simple if you follow the directions … old world Pagan spell …

question::::to the old and to the new … if your searching for something other then what you believe in now or are just searching for something period … you came to the right place … you first need to ask yourself a question … do I believe in something greater then myself … lots of people say they are spiritual but don't..they say they are their own Higher Power … well good luck to them … if you are of a religious faction, no matter what it is and your searching for somet … hing better for whatever your reason..you must not be satisfied where you are right now … you are not alone..many come here to my groups in search of these things … being spiritual is a lifestyle as much as anything else and we have no books to follow like other religions do … we all have different ideas on what it is to be spiritual but we have basic ideas … love and kindness,,,compassion,,,sharing, and all the other great things that go along with these … now my question to you is:::::::do you want to put in the effort to learn and find your path and live this way??????

Question:::::now things happen in life that may make you angry or hate someone … this is a fact … and when they do this for whatever reason you are not in control of your life … I know it's very hard to be spiritual and have unconditional love for these people … I have learned to deal with it in my own way … this is to say I don't even let them make me angry or hate them … this is not easy and it took years to learn how to do this … when I pass on to the Higher Power, I will not take any baggage with me … my question is:::::can anyone out there do the same??????

Question:::::now spiritual people use many things for personal and home protection … I have not cleansed my home for a long time and spells they wear off … but, I have tinas alter … I cleaned it and organized it and then asked the Higher Power to let it be used as a protection for the house … this is where I do my work when helping people with there spiritual problems … and all my kids are protected by spells created right there at the altar when outside the house … but some spiritual people think that just because they think their protected by doing nothing but being spiritual … .believe me, I have been attacked a lot of times without protection … darkness will seek out the light to try and destroy it at every turn … my question to you is:::::what do you do to protect your home and self and loved ones?????

_____
_____
_____
_____
_____
_____
_____
_____
_____
_____
_____
_____
_____
_____
_____
_____
_____
_____
_____
_____
_____
_____

question::::so who are we ... are we religious and follow a bible and a god who destroys his own children ... .are we spiritual that when it comes down to battles we run off because we believe not to battle, but to love and think that will win ... are we the chosen one who have special powers given to us by the devine to help those in need ... are we old world pagans who still use spells to get things done ... are we new wave wiccans who basically don't know shit, because they took all their learning from the old ones and don't really know how to use it ... are we the ones who can enable us to use our soul force to change things when needed ... .my question to you is:::::::you call yourself spiritual, just what are you???????

Question:::::don't you just love those out there that think their Holier then you, in some way or the other … hey mom and dad, you passed over..what do you think … … and I'm talking spiritual here … people who act like they have all the answers and have ascended all the way up, and their still alive..or the young one who says they saw the light and now knows it all … .interesting, isn't it … but then you look a little closer and find they can't even keep their own life in order … lolol … .what a wonder it must be to have all the knowledge of everything while still here … they must be doing everything for everyone, with powers like that … .meeting them would be like looking into the face of the Higher Power … … my question is:::::do you or did you ever know someone like this??????

Question:::::have anyone out there ever had a temporary disconnection to the Higher Power and didn't know why, when nothing changed with what they were doing??????

_____

_____

_____

_____

_____

_____

_____

_____

_____

_____

_____

_____

_____

_____

_____

_____

_____

_____

_____

_____

_____

_____

_____

_____

_____

_____

_____

_____

_____

_____

Question:::::ok, lets be honest here for a moment ... I know we talked a little about spiritual books ... I believe that all spiritual books of any kind can give you some information ... but beware them if you are just starting out into being spiritual ... you might find yourself falling prey to the ideas and start following them because you have nothing else to cling to ... this would be a mistake ... don't forget it is YOU who chooses YOUR own path ... spiritual books are 99.9% written ... to get you to follow their way of thinking ... when is the last time that you read a spiritual book of any kind that didn't tell you to do or be anything ... they all do ..and I'm sorry to say their are too many out there that are just frauds also ... spirituality is a growing and expanding lifestyle and everyone wants to get in on the $$$$$$$ it can bring one with a book ... they probably make up most of the shit in it any way ... so my question to you is:::::what would you recommend to the people who are just getting started into spirituality?????

_____
_____
_____
_____
_____
_____
_____
_____
_____
_____
_____
_____
_____
_____
_____
_____
_____
_____
_____
_____
_____

Question:::::now MR Coffee makes a great item … a coffee pot that not only brews a great coffee but is at a very reasonable price … but of course this is not about coffee..lol … this about spiritual books … some people think the more expensive it is the better it is as with all things we buy … and then after they buy it and read it maybe they get a few things out of it that they could have gotten on these groups … without paying anything..lol … so my question to you is:::::how many times have you went out and bought a spiritual book only to have read it and wished you could get your money back??????

Question:::::ok, lets be honest here for a moment ... I know we talked a little about spiritual books ... I believe that all spiritual books of any kind can give you some information ... but beware them if you are just starting out into being spiritual ... you might find yourself falling prey to the ideas and start following them because you have nothing else to cling to ... this would be a mistake ... don't forget it is YOU who chooses YOUR own path ... spiritual books are 99.9% written ... to get you to follow their way of thinking ... when is the last time that you read a spiritual book of any kind that didn't tell you to do or be anything ... they all do ..and I'm sorry to say their are too many out there that are just frauds also ... spirituality is a growing and expanding lifestyle and everyone wants to get in on the $$$$$$$ it can bring one with a book ... they probably make up most of the shit in it any way ... so my question to you is:::::what would you recommend to the people who are just getting started into spirituality?????

_____
_____
_____
_____
_____
_____
_____
_____
_____
_____
_____
_____
_____
_____
_____
_____
_____
_____
_____
_____
_____
_____
_____

Question:::::question and comments … sometimes I post comments ..but if you notice I never say anything like this is the TRUTH … .that's because everyone has their own truth until they meet someone with a similar truth … I always say, this is what I believe … .but for my questions, one of the reasons I post them is to see other spiritual answers so I can grow my personal knowledge and expand and strengthen my path with your answers that are not mine … I always have a personal answer to my questions … remember I said one of my reasons???my question is what do you think the main reason I have for posting my questions????????

_____
_____
_____
_____
_____
_____
_____
_____
_____
_____
_____
_____
_____
_____
_____
_____
_____
_____
_____
_____
_____
_____
_____
_____
_____
_____

Questions::::yes plural..I am going to try something a little different today with this post … usually, I blab a lot and then get to the question..and I am very happy with the feedback comments on my groups..but today I will be blabbing.lol and have more then one question within this post … I am trying to get more people responding to my posts by doing this with more then one question … so let's see what happens … vibrations … .everyone and everything has a different one, but …, some are so close together that we can see and hear the other things that are close to our vibration … take the earth for example … it has a vibration soooo close to all living things on it we can see them … question::::::;do you believe this last statement or do you have a different opinion?????now again, our vibration is such that there are certain things we can't see or hear … for instance, demons and angels … if we could change our vibration to theirs or theirs to ours would we be able to see them and them us and communicate?????and then again can being in a certain state of vibration protect us from the darkness and let in the light???????

question:::::::since according to one of my recent questions, most believe there can be no mortal Master of spirituality on this earth ..and I hope we all spiritual people strive to have understanding and knowledge while were here.my question is :::::will there come a time before you pass on that you can say your truly happy with your knowledge and ability to help others, or will you go out with something inside you empty?????????

now many people have many different gifts … some more then one … and some none at all … some are learning them and some are afraid of them..my question to you is:::::what do you believe to be the most powerful gift one can have???????

_____
_____
_____
_____
_____
_____
_____
_____
_____
_____
_____
_____
_____
_____
_____
_____
_____
_____
_____
_____
_____
_____
_____
_____
_____
_____
_____
_____
_____
_____

comment:::::since so many people seem not to understand my post about the fisherman, I will say this … too many people who claim to be spiritual think all they have to do is help and their job is done and over … sorry, it's not … we are responsible for anything that happens because of our choices or actions, with anyone … .whether it be simple or complicated … example..your walking down the street and a beggar is on the corner..you want to give him some money..but as you ap … proach you notice the stench of alcohol coming off him … .if you give him the money and say, well I helped, and he buys a bottle with it and walks out drunk in front of the bus and gets killed … is it not part of your fault … don't even bother trying to talk your way out of the situation to make yourself not guilty … … this is how I'm finding more and more spiritual people acting … not ever responsible for their choices and actions … well you don't have to comment. You know who you are … spend your time trying to squeeze yourself into a righteous place … goodnite and may your Higher Power go with you and yours>>>>>

question::::do you ever get the feeling that being spiritual ain't worth a shit ... nothing ever works for you no matter how much you talk to your Higher Power ... you are sooo close to losing your faith its ridiculous ... .you look around and see the haves and the have nots .and wonder why you ain't one of the haves ... .but then again you notice that nothing bad ever happens to you ..you never have a battle ... you think your special and above all that crap..you think you got it all working for you.. never a problem, so you think your soo spiritual you don't have to fear anything ... well yes there are you that are like that and live that life ... but my question is:::::what about the rest of us who have to fight every day to uphold our spiritual ... what are we???????

_____
_____
_____
_____
_____
_____
_____
_____
_____
_____
_____
_____
_____
_____
_____
_____
_____
_____
_____
_____
_____
_____
_____
_____

question::::now I read here a lot on spiritual awakening … some even ask how to do it..well we know it's different for everyone and some never do … but I believe it's also a different kind of awakening for everyone..no 2 people have the same one..that's what's great about it … being individual but part of the whole..now my question to you is:::::what was your individual awakening if you have had it yet?????

_____
_____
_____
_____
_____
_____
_____
_____
_____
_____
_____
_____
_____
_____
_____
_____
_____
_____
_____
_____
_____
_____
_____
_____
_____

question:::::now good old Webster defines a path as a route which someone follows or progresses ... sounds about right..but let's look at it more closely ... I believe a path should encompass all that you can accumulate spiritually wise as long as you live..a path just doesn't just have to be one line for instance ... imagine if you will..a seed of a tree planted ... when it takes root it starts to grow above the ground ... and as it grows or matures it starts to send out branches and ... leaves ... now each of these could be called a different path..but I belief that all the branches are part of the original path ... each holding its own information and by being part of the trunk or branch it sprouted from is in actuality a part of the path ... now imagine the tree a hundred yrs old..all that information being part of a single path ... this is what I believe for us..we should never say someone elses path does not concern us ..and we have our own ... that is why when someone else comes along with a different idea I always say its possible ... because maybe in the future it may hold information I will need ... so this is a path to me ... an ever changing and growing from the original and encompassing ALL information we can get while still around on this rock we call earth ... I would be interested in knowing what you believe to be a path??????

_____
_____
_____
_____
_____
_____
_____
_____
_____
_____
_____
_____
_____
_____
_____
_____
_____
_____

question:::::why is it that soooo many people say they are spiritual also say there way is the only way …????????

Question:::::now a rose by any other name is still a rose ... and over the ages we have called different beings or things by different names..God, source, universe, Higher Power and etc ... but what about the people who also believe in lower beings or things like gods and goddesses ... for instance, gaia as mother earth or fire or water etc ... my question is ::::do you have names of them you believe in that are below the Higher Power, but are still powerfull???????

Question:::::spiritual rituals … from the beginning of mankind, there was spiritualism … when man found out how to use fire, they started a connection with their Higher Power and thanked it for what they received … they performed rituals to honor their Higher Power for the gifts … as time moved forward more and more groups of people did the same when they received gifts … it was a spiritual world back then … then came modernized religion and started forced changes in these … groups … Catholicism stole from the pagans and gnostics and anyone else they wanted to be in control them..they even went so far as to try and destroy them … but these people still had their beliefs and rituals … now even to this day they still exist and perform rituals … but somewhere along the line some found out they no longer had to perform rituals because they had the connection to their Higher Power and only need ask for what they wanted … .my wife used to say rituals were all pageantry, but, if they wanted to then it may have helped them strengthen their beliefs … .she still performed rituals herself … I myself have moved on from that … as in my healings I just ask my Higher Power to use me as a conduit to heal … my question is:::::::as a spiritual person do you still perform rituals for what you want to do or get????????

question:::::now I see all kinds of spiritual people on my groups … and most are of the same mind … all believing and following the basics … but there are those who seem to choose to be different and still call themselves spiritual because they say their on their own path … my question is:::::I believe in separate paths but don't we need to all be on the same page in order to spread the word and try to make this rock a better place to live???????

question::::now spiritual people don't look at death or leaving this plane of existence as something bad ... like the Irish do, they party for the person who is gone, so as to help them cross over to the next life ... .now as I believe the departed has choices they can make(free will and all) ... they can choose to stick around or not ... I would never want someone to stick around, unless they wanted to ... I would prefer they move on to better things in their new plane of existence ... I believe if needed they can come back and help..but then again it's there choice ... my question to you is ::::::what do you believe about this??????

Question:::::now many people have said all the answers you need are within you ... I disagree..are minds are not that great to hold all the answers ... I believe that the questions are answered by the higher Power to your mind so that's why you would think that ... and also in the simple way that your mind is capable of understanding ... we all can't be Einstein.lol ... but regardless, how can we get anything if not connected to the Higher Power ... and that brings us to the how ... so ... me meditate ..some use alcohol or medication, or drugs to reach that place where they have total connection ... I my self get my answers through my dreams, but occasionally love to drink my beer and get into that relaxed state of mind to make a direct connection ... .then the questions are asked and the answers flow freely back to me ... so, before judging anyone on how they get the answers, my question is :::::how do you get your answers to your questions????????

_____
_____
_____
_____
_____
_____
_____
_____
_____
_____
_____
_____
_____
_____
_____
_____
_____
_____
_____
_____
_____

Question:::::now I know I have a lot of religious people on my groups … they consider themselves spiritual, but will never let go of their bibles and religious beliefs … .not to start an argument, just a fact, that I have noticed … .so my question to you is::::when your religion takes in children to give them bible study … why is there never any mention of the old testament of the god who was so malevolent he destroyed his own children,,,for whatever reason????? and keep in mind I went to sunday school and there all alike question:::::now some of you say LOVE is the answer to all … and it can overcome all … well ponder this::::were back in the 60's..the time of free love and the spirituality is there … you have a peacefull protest..but the government doesn't like it so there are armed police and others that say you must stop … so being one who believes love can stop them, you take an arm full of flowers and advance towards them … they tell you to stop many times but you don't … so they shoot you dead … now your just a dead person … you will be mourned, but, where did the love change anything … .my question is ::::tell me story about yourself where love alone changed something?????

Question:::Now a couple yrs ago, on one of my groups, white light energy, we had healing sessions ... myself along with some others would heal people in real time ... everybody had a different way to do it ... of course sometimes things were beyond our control..but mostly we could help people some permanently, some for a while, and a few not at all for whatever reason ... my point before my question is I believe all knew they didn't do it alone ... as with me there was a connection betwe ... en A, my Higher Power, and C, the one to be healed ... that was me, B..I never claimed to be the healer, just gifted with the ability to connect the 2 ... why, I don't really know to this day why I was chosen amongst a lot of others around the world to be able to do this ... now I have always known I had a connection between me and some kind of Higher Power, before I even called it that ... my question to you is:::::is there anyone out there who believes they can do anything supernatural without the help and or guidance of their Higher Power, whatever you may want to call it??????

question::::::now people are always talking about changing frequency … for many different reasons … I don't worry about doing that because when I speak with my Higher Power,,all frequencies are there, as the answers to my questions … and as far as changing myself to interact with other beings and people, it is always natural … yes I believe in changing frequencies for certain purposes, but it becomes very easy when you do it with your Higher Power … now my question is::::how do you change your frequency??????

Question:::::energy, science has proven it exists, but we knew this way before science did ... there is more then 1 kind ... we have energy in batteries ... we can harness it from the sun cleanly ... and then there is ours ... the energy that keeps the body alive ... without it we would just die away ... .my question is :::::does energy change temperature like the body does or does it remain a constant of its own????????

Question:::::now MR Coffee makes a great item … a coffee pot that not only brews a great coffee but is at a very reasonable price … but of course this is not about coffee..lol … this about spiritual books … some people think the more expensive it is the better it is as with all things we buy … and then after they buy it and read it maybe they get a few things out of it that they could have gotten on these groups … .without paying anything..lol … so my question to you is:::::how many times have you went out and bought a spiritual book only to have read it and wished you could get your money back??????

Question::::::::What yes or no pendulum questions do U have about ET's, spirits, & other planets? from mr whitly ... check it out ... now I have been aware of this con for decades ... I asked him 2 questions and he got 1 wrong..lol ... ... then he decided to tell me I asked the question the wrong way ... a question is a question, no???????I proceeded to tell him that a real seer would have answers to the questions and not just yes or no ... .he claims to be 62 so if that's true, he should know better then to try and con someone ... lolol, go check out the post and all that is commented under before I ask you my question ... ... my question is, when is the last time you found a fraud doing the same thing and fell or almost fell for it??????

Question:::::a 2 edged sword can cut both ways … .so when you swing it you have to know exactly what your doing … just like being spiritual … when you give people answers when trying to help you must be careful not to cut the wrong person … … you must really think about what advice you are going to give … what works for you might not work for them … especially if their new to being spiritual … they may be very vulnerable to outside influences, both good and bad … so you have to go back in your mind and think about what got you where you are today … you may have been stronger then them and able to understand the idea of real spiritualism … .but they may not be … so my question to you is:::::::when and if you give spiritual advice do you think about what I just said before doing it???????

_____
_____
_____
_____
_____
_____
_____
_____
_____
_____
_____
_____
_____
_____
_____
_____
_____
_____
_____
_____
_____
_____
_____

Question::::I have never said that I am anything more then a mortal man in quest of the spiritual truth ... and each of us has their own ... but there have been some on my groups that say they are masters in spirituality..and you have seen their comments ... and those that say they know the REAL spiritual truth ... and then there are those that claim to believe in those that were spiritual masters, even religious ones ... my question to you is::::::do you think as a mortal being, anyone can know it all and be a spiritual master?????and remember, religiously, even jesus was a mortal being ....

---

question::::a little while ago my 12 yr old and I were in the kitchen … he was supposed to take his cough medicine, and was trying to change subjects thinking I would forget.lolol … we were joking around and I told him I wasn't so stupid for him to try and do that and if he didn't take it I would bring down upon him the wrath of Satan himself … he started laughing and then I did because, as a spiritual person as was his mom, we taught him there is no satan … he believes in a … ngels and demons and light and dark … and he knows are home is protected from the darkness … he is gifted and has been seeing things for about the last few yrs … which we explain to him depending on what he sees … anyway I told him I would post this and ask a question … he can't wait to see … so my question is:::::::do any opf you out there have children who the situation is similar to??????

_____
_____
_____
_____
_____
_____
_____
_____
_____
_____
_____
_____
_____
_____
_____
_____
_____
_____
_____
_____
_____
_____

Question:::::ok, lets be honest here for a moment ... I know we talked a little about spiritual books ... I believe that all spiritual books of any kind can give you some information ... but beware them if you are just starting out into being spiritual ... you might find yourself falling prey to the ideas and start following them because you have nothing else to cling to ... this would be a mistake ... don't forget it is YOU who chooses YOUR own path ... spiritual books are 99.9% written ... to get you to follow their way of thinking ... when is the last time that you read a spiritual book of any kind that didn't tell you to do or be anything ... they all do ..and I'm sorry to say their are too many out there that are just frauds also ... spirituality is a growing and expanding lifestyle and everyone wants to get in on the $$$$$$$ it can bring one with a book ... they probably make up most of the shit in it any way ... so my question to you is:::::what would you recommend to the people who are just getting started into spirituality????

_____

_____

_____

_____

_____

_____

_____

_____

_____

_____

_____

_____

_____

_____

_____

_____

_____

_____

_____

_____

_____

_____

_____

_____

Printed in the United States
By Bookmasters

Question:::::ok, lets be honest here for a moment ... I know we talked a little about spiritual books ... I believe that all spiritual books of any kind can give you some information ... but beware them if you are just starting out into being spiritual ... you might find yourself falling prey to the ideas and start following them because you have nothing else to cling to ... this would be a mistake ... don't forget it is YOU who chooses YOUR own path ... spiritual books are 99.9% written ... to get you to follow their way of thinking ... when is the last time that you read a spiritual book of any kind that didn't tell you to do or be anything ... they all do ..and I'm sorry to say their are too many out there that are just frauds also ... spirituality is a growing and expanding lifestyle and everyone wants to get in on the $$$$$$$ it can bring one with a book ... they probably make up most of the shit in it any way ... so my question to you is:::::what would you recommend to the people who are just getting started into spirituality????

Printed in the United States
By Bookmasters